Walter P. Chrysler Museum

Walter P. Chrysler Museum

Forward: *The American Heritage of DaimlerChrysler*

Produced by Zenda Inc.

for **DaimlerChrysler Corporation**

Contents

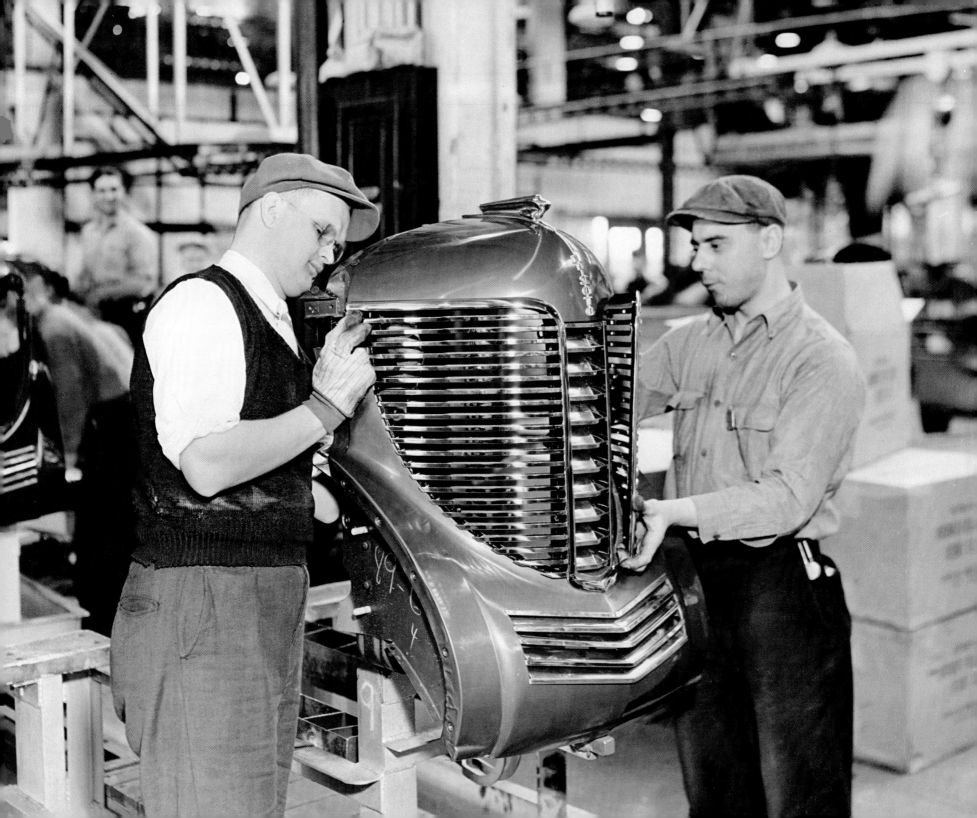

Acknowledgments

ALL BOOKS are collaborative efforts but none more so than those built on museum exhibitions, which are themselves by their very nature collaborative. This work simply would not have been possible without the cooperation of the folks at Design Craftsman and Chedd-Angier, who shared the research and imagery they used in creating the Walter P. Chrysler Museum's exhibitions. These served as a starting point for building and as a baseline for producing the story told here. In turn, neither their work nor ours would have been possible without the researchers and archivists at the DaimlerChrysler Corporate Historical Collection in Auburn Hills, Michigan, home of so many of the images and so much of the information included here. Especially in their determination to dispel the myths, misconceptions and misinformation about Chrysler's past and to make sure that we, at least, got it right did this tiny but dedicated band serve to make this book better.

Several people, with a long record of service at Chrysler, a vast knowledge of the Corporation's history and a profound understanding of the significance of the story, had a more direct impact on the narrative that follows. Alfred D. Bosley, Bruce Thomas and Eugene Weiss read every word of the text (including the captions), checked, challenged and commented on a number of them in the name of accuracy and truth and in general made sure that what we said was what we meant, which is no mean feat for a work seeking to recount so broad a story in so tight a context. Not only are we grateful to them for helping us to avoid errors of fact and interpretation but we salute them for their passion and precision. Also improving the text were those who read the manuscript with an eye toward polishing the language in which the tale unfolded. Our thanks to Judith Dressel, especially, and to Patricia Hogan and Philip George for helping make sure our sentences flowed, our language matched our intent, the words we used were the words we should have used and what we said made sense to readers who had never engineered a car or a corporate takeover.

Foreword

WHEN THE WALTER P. CHRYSLER MUSEUM opened in October 1999, it was a remarkable achievement. Incredibly, it was the first time that an active American auto manufacturer had created its own museum. The tens of thousands of visitors have expressed surprise and delight that the Museum is not a predictable display of beautifully restored old cars, or a razzle-dazzle exercise in brand marketing. Instead the Museum is a beautifully designed building with an exhibition that carefully interprets the history of one of the world's most colorful automobile companies. The story is told with great cars and with photographs, interactive exhibits, video and sound presentations and authentic vignettes. The result is richly nostalgic and potently educational.

The Museum could not help being a success. The employees of Chrysler Corporation always had a special feeling about their Company and its history and for years dreamed that one day there would be a museum devoted to Chrysler Corporation and its products. Once work began, it became a labor of love. Executives worked with the designers of the building. Engineers steeped in the Company's history debated which cars best represent the Chrysler story and began acquiring and restoring those cars the Company did not already own. Other employees worked with Museum designers to outline the Company's history for the Museum exhibition.

As the effort to create the Museum reached the final stages, a company that had been a product of mergers during its long history merged again, this time with the most historic of companies, Daimler-Benz, becoming DaimlerChrysler. History may be a continuum, but it is also a record of change over time. In 1998, one historical era closed and another began. The core exhibition at the Museum gained a title—*Forward*—and a subtitle *The American Heritage of DaimlerChrysler.* Other than that, the thrust and the contents of the Museum were unchanged.

The Museum appeals to everyone. It is lively and colorful, nostalgic and factual, technical and accessible, fun and educational, suitable for young and old. It pays tribute to Chrysler's storied past. A unique dimension of the Museum—and of DaimlerChrysler employees—is the fact that hundreds, active and retired, volunteer to serve as hosts and guides. Judging by the comments from visitors, many of whom come thousands of miles to pay homage to cars they love, the experience *is* special. This warm human element is appropriate for a museum that bears the name of Walter P. Chrysler, an automotive genius known all his life as a warm and friendly man.

These pages attempt to condense the Museum's contents and the Company's history into a portable form that preserves the flavor of the exhibition and tells the story of a remarkable company's history.

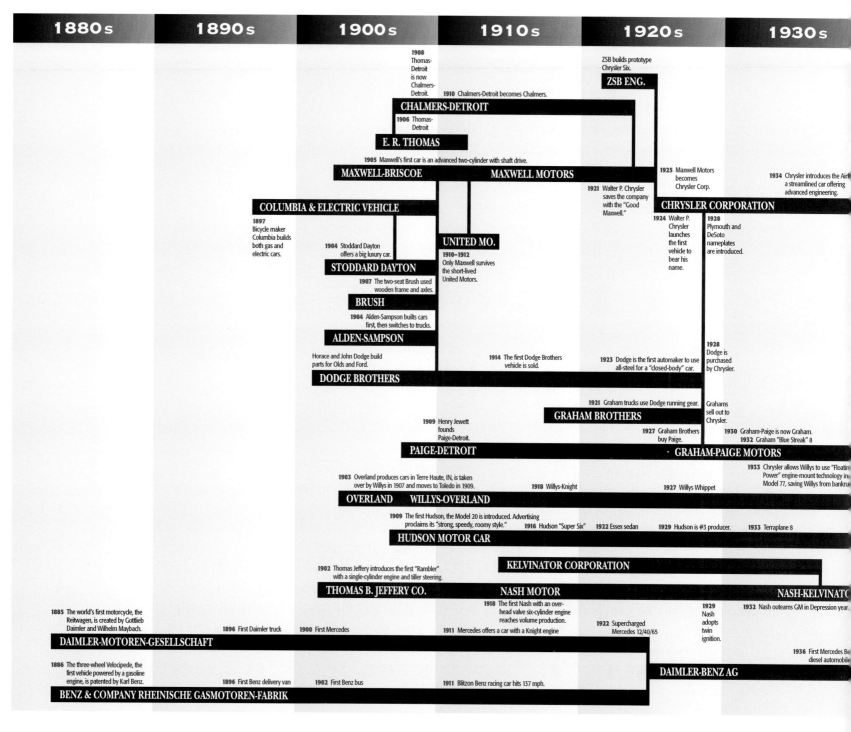

1880s | **1890s** | **1900s** | **1910s** | **1920s** | **1930s**

1908 Thomas-Detroit is now Chalmers-Detroit.

ZSB builds prototype Chrysler Six.

ZSB ENG.

1910 Chalmers-Detroit becomes Chalmers.

CHALMERS-DETROIT

1906 Thomas-Detroit

E. R. THOMAS

1905 Maxwell's first car is an advanced two-cylinder with shaft drive.

MAXWELL-BRISCOE | **MAXWELL MOTORS**

1925 Maxwell Motors becomes Chrysler Corp.

1934 Chrysler introduces the Airfl a streamlined car offering advanced engineering.

1921 Walter P. Chrysler saves the company with the "Good Maxwell."

CHRYSLER CORPORATION

COLUMBIA & ELECTRIC VEHICLE

1897 Bicycle maker Columbia builds both gas and electric cars.

1924 Walter P. Chrysler launches the first vehicle to bear his name.

1928 Plymouth and DeSoto nameplates are introduced.

1904 Stoddard Dayton offers a big luxury car.

UNITED MO.

1910–1912 Only Maxwell survives the short-lived United Motors.

STODDARD DAYTON

1907 The two-seat Brush used wooden frame and axles.

BRUSH

1904 Alden-Sampson builts cars first, then switches to trucks.

1928 Dodge is purchased by Chrysler.

ALDEN-SAMPSON

Horace and John Dodge build parts for Olds and Ford.

1914 The first Dodge Brothers vehicle is sold.

1923 Dodge is the first automaker to use all-steel for a "closed-body" car.

DODGE BROTHERS

1921 Graham trucks use Dodge running gear.

GRAHAM BROTHERS

Grahams sell out to Chrysler.

1909 Henry Jewett founds Paige-Detroit.

1927 Graham Brothers buy Paige.

1930 Graham-Paige is now Graham.
1932 Graham "Blue Streak" 8

PAIGE-DETROIT | **· GRAHAM-PAIGE MOTORS**

1933 Chrysler allows Willys to use "Floatin Power" engine-mount technology in Model 77, saving Willys from bankru

1903 Overland produces cars in Terre Haute, IN, is taken over by Willys in 1907 and moves to Toledo in 1909.

1918 Willys-Knight

1927 Willys Whippet

OVERLAND | **WILLYS-OVERLAND**

1909 The first Hudson, the Model 20 is introduced. Advertising proclaims its "strong, speedy, roomy style."

1916 Hudson "Super Six"

1922 Essex sedan

1929 Hudson is #3 producer.

1933 Terraplane 8

HUDSON MOTOR CAR

KELVINATOR CORPORATION

1902 Thomas Jeffery introduces the first "Rambler" with a single-cylinder engine and tiller steering.

THOMAS B. JEFFERY CO. | **NASH MOTOR**

NASH-KELVINATO

1918 The first Nash with an overhead valve six-cylinder engine reaches volume production.

1929 Nash adopts twin ignition.

1932 Nash outearns GM in Depression year.

1885 The world's first motorcycle, the Reitwagen, is created by Gottlieb Daimler and Wilhelm Maybach.

1896 First Daimler truck

1900 First Mercedes

1911 Mercedes offers a car with a Knight engine

1922 Supercharged Mercedes 12/40/65

DAIMLER-MOTOREN-GESELLSCHAFT

1936 First Mercedes Be diesel automobile

1886 The three-wheel Velocipede, the first vehicle powered by a gasoline engine, is patented by Karl Benz.

1896 First Benz delivery van

1902 First Benz bus

1911 Blitzen Benz racing car hits 137 mph.

DAIMLER-BENZ AG

BENZ & COMPANY RHEINISCHE GASMOTOREN-FABRIK

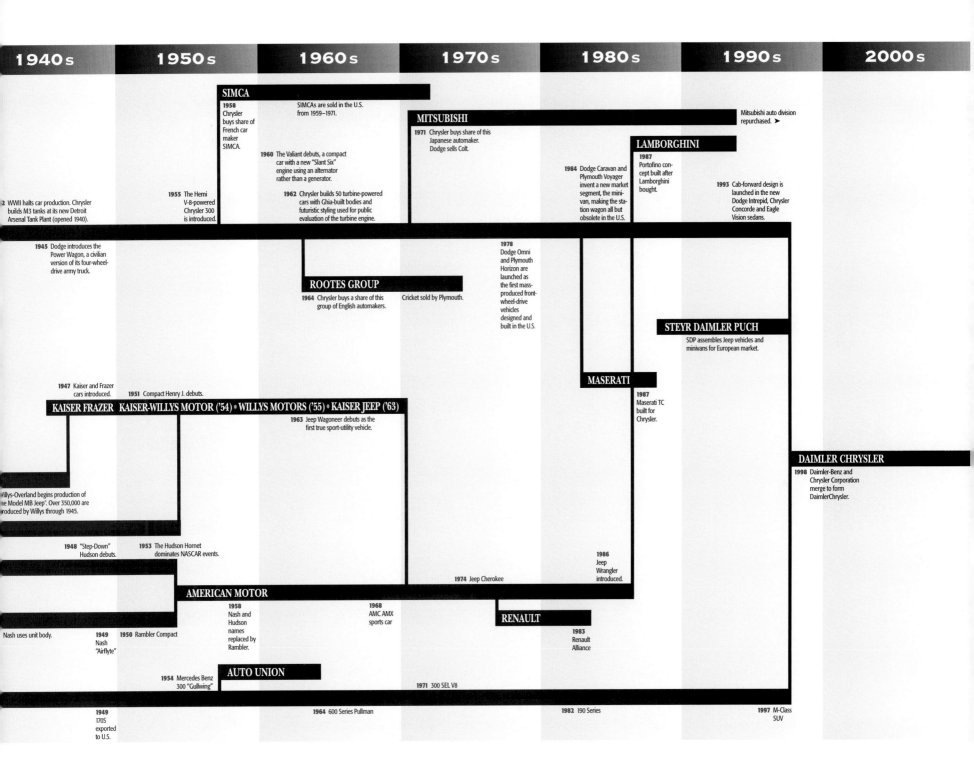

SIMCA

1958 Chrysler buys share of French car maker SIMCA.

SIMCAs are sold in the U.S. from 1959–1971.

MITSUBISHI

1971 Chrysler buys share of this Japanese automaker. Dodge sells Colt.

Mitsubishi auto division repurchased. ➤

LAMBORGHINI

1987 Portofino concept built after Lamborghini bought.

1960 The Valiant debuts, a compact car with a new "Slant Six" engine using an alternator rather than a generator.

1984 Dodge Caravan and Plymouth Voyager invent a new market segment, the minivan, making the station wagon all but obsolete in the U.S.

1993 Cab-forward design is launched in the new Dodge Intrepid, Chrysler Concorde and Eagle Vision sedans.

1955 The Hemi V-8-powered Chrysler 300 is introduced.

1962 Chrysler builds 50 turbine-powered cars with Ghia-built bodies and futuristic styling used for public evaluation of the turbine engine.

2 WWII halts car production. Chrysler builds M3 tanks at its new Detroit Arsenal Tank Plant (opened 1940).

1945 Dodge introduces the Power Wagon, a civilian version of its four-wheel-drive army truck.

1978 Dodge Omni and Plymouth Horizon are launched as the first mass-produced front-wheel-drive vehicles designed and built in the U.S.

ROOTES GROUP

1964 Chrysler buys a share of this group of English automakers.

Cricket sold by Plymouth.

STEYR DAIMLER PUCH

SDP assembles Jeep vehicles and minivans for European market.

MASERATI

1987 Maserati TC built for Chrysler.

1947 Kaiser and Frazer cars introduced.

1951 Compact Henry J. debuts.

KAISER FRAZER   **KAISER-WILLYS MOTOR ('54) • WILLYS MOTORS ('55) • KAISER JEEP ('63)**

1963 Jeep Wagoneer debuts as the first true sport-utility vehicle.

DAIMLER CHRYSLER

1998 Daimler-Benz and Chrysler Corporation merge to form DaimlerChrysler.

Willys-Overland begins production of the Model MB Jeep®. Over 350,000 are produced by Willys through 1945.

1948 "Step-Down" Hudson debuts.

1953 The Hudson Hornet dominates NASCAR events.

1986 Jeep Wrangler introduced.

1974 Jeep Cherokee

AMERICAN MOTOR

1958 Nash and Hudson names replaced by Rambler.

1968 AMC AMX sports car

RENAULT

Nash uses unit body.

1949 Nash "Airflyte"

1950 Rambler Compact

1983 Renault Alliance

1954 Mercedes Benz 300 "Gullwing"

AUTO UNION

1971 300 SEL V8

1949 170S exported to U.S.

1964 600 Series Pullman

1982 190 Series

1997 M-Class SUV

American Progress

As THE 20TH CENTURY OPENED, a young railroad machinist from Kansas named Walter P. Chrysler was living in Salt Lake City working in the Denver & Rio Grande Railroad roundhouse, happily moving ahead in his chosen career and newly married. Son of a locomotive engineer, Chrysler had grown up being in love with trains, as many men born in the latter part of the 19th century were. In a young country still consumed with settling its vast interior, trains were quite literally engines of progress, symbolizing modernity, power, technological progress and the conquest of time and distance. For a nation that only celebrated its centennial the year after Chrysler's birth, railroads had literally forged national ties. Railroads would continue to expand well into the new century, with miles of track peaking in the 1920s. Railroads and urban and interurban rail systems determined where towns grew, how cities developed and how far people could live from work and play.

But it was *mass* transportation. It took people where they wanted to go, if where they wanted to go was where the rails went, and it took them there according to its own schedule, not on the whim of the user. The 19th century, styled the age of steam, still relied on the horse as personal transport until the bicycle appeared in its last decades. What had been perfected as the "safety" bicycle quickly became a national fad. It was a novelty—mechanical, *personal* transportation, a clean, fast, easy-to-operate device that could take you anywhere you wanted to go when you wanted to go there. With its popularity there grew up a generation of bicycle parts makers and

mechanics, accustomed to metal fabrication, bearings, gears, lubrication and rubber tires.

Even as the bicycle was making people aware that personal transportation was a possibility, a new mode of transport made its first appearance. The development of a four-cycle internal combustion engine in Germany in the 1870s was quickly followed by refinements that improved efficiency and reliability and reduced engine weight. By the mid-1880s, Gottlieb Daimler and Karl Benz had developed engines light enough to propel vehicles. Even at that embryonic stage, it was apparent that once this power source was perfected, it would offer significant advantages over steam power or battery-powered electric motors as a means of powering personal transportation. These European developments were reported to mechanically inclined Americans like Walter Chrysler via journals such as *Scientific American*—distributed by a railway-based postal system. By the 1890s, inspired tinkerers all across the United States were trying to build their versions of what the French had dubbed the "automobile."

Inevitably, a couple of bicycle mechanics did it first. Frank and Charles Duryea, brothers working in Chicopee, Massachusetts, managed to put an automobile on the road in 1893. Close on their heels was Elwood P. Haynes in Indiana. By 1896, Charles Brady King built and drove a car through the streets of Detroit, accompanied by a friend riding a bicycle. The friend, named Henry Ford, was an engineer at the local Edison generating plant. He would have an automobile of his own in a few months. He also had something

simple, affordable vehicle in volume and Henry Ford's determination to give the farmer a tool to ease rural drudgery and isolation came the American automobile industry. It rapidly became a phenomenon that would eclipse its European roots in the first decade of the new century.

Americans everywhere took to the new contraptions, which many saw as yet another example of modern progress, right in line with electric lighting, telephones, motion pictures and the airplane (one more wonder produced by former bicycle mechanics). In fact, progress was the buzzword of the decade. The new president, Theodore Roosevelt, the youngest man so far to sit in the White House, called himself a Progressive, and his followers wanted to improve everything from city government to local roads to the morals of the loose-living. Progressive social workers opened homes for the impoverished in city slums while Progressive journalists—called muckrakers—attacked the excesses of big corporations and called for safe foods and the regulation of drugs and patent medicines. Prosperous and industrious, expansive and optimistic, Americans embraced such progress, and soon they were not only pinging and banging their way along the country's dusty and muddy highways in any variety of automobiles but also making up songs to sing about the experience. Among their number was the young railroad machinist, Walter Chrysler, who in 1908 begged and borrowed the money he needed to buy his first car—a huge, brass-bound, ivory-colored beauty he had come across and fallen for, head over heels, in Chicago while traveling in his job.

By that year, the American auto industry was producing thousands of cars in dozens of makes all across the country. The cars came in all sizes, shapes, prices and mechanical configurations. The Olds Motor Works

else—a distaste, acquired firsthand, for the isolation and unremitting labor of farm life that later would determine his destiny as an automobile manufacturer in the new century. By 1898, a maker of steam and gasoline engines named Ransom E. Olds had started selling automobiles in Detroit, when a factory fire forced him to concentrate all production on his simplest and cheapest model, a model easy to build in volume. From Ransom Olds's early success in building a

had become a vast training ground for the future leaders in auto manufacture, including many—such as John and Horace Dodge and Roy Chapin—with a place in our story. Henry Ford was getting ready to introduce the Model T, a car that quickly became a sensation—a fully equipped full-sized touring car for the unheard of low price of $850 "F.O.B. Detroit." Sixty miles north of where Henry Ford was building Model Ts, a former carriage manufacturer named William C. Durant was profiting with a car produced bearing David Buick's name. Durant's goal was to dominate the new auto industry the way he had once dominated carriage manufacture, and his idea was to consolidate the industry by using a combine. In 1908, he incorporated his combine, which he called General Motors. By then, some 500 companies were making cars in cities around the country, but the biggest—like Ford and General Motors—remained centered in and around Detroit, where Ransom Olds had built his first factory.

Soon these companies would begin to merge and buy each other out or falter and go bankrupt, but through it all, new cars, improved cars, faster cars would keep rolling onto showroom floors as Americans bought them in ever greater numbers. For by 1908, the auto itself had become an American institution. The names of automobile pioneers—the Apperson brothers, the Duryea brothers, Elwood P. Haynes, Charles Brady King, James Ward Packard, Albert A. Pope, Alexander Winton—were being added to the annals of American progress. Some automakers were even beginning to make the kinds of fortunes that Americans associated with the old railroad barons and captains of industry from the 19th century. One day, Walter Chrysler would join the roll call of these new 20th-century moguls. He would become a world leader in

the manufacture of automobiles bearing his own name, in an ascent accomplished remarkably quickly and at a time when it was thought such achievements were no longer possible.

But in 1908, he was just a young man in love with a pretty car.

In the first decade of the 20th century, the well-dressed female automobilist wore on a typical Sunday outing clothes styled to cover as much as possible, not so much out of modesty as to avoid currents of cold air and the splatterings of mud and muck in winter and choking dust and the smacking of small insects in summer.

1886

■ German engineers Gottlieb Daimler and William Maybach produce the world's first gas-powered autocar.

■ Another German, Karl Benz, patents the first gasoline-powered vehicle based on something other than a horse-drawn carriage, traditionally marking the "birthday" of the gasoline automobile.

1894

▼ Benz's Velo becomes the world's first production car.

1897

■ Albert Augustus Pope begins manufacturing gas and electric cars in America under the brand name Columbia.

1898

■ The United States goes to war with Spain, trumpeting its entry onto the stage of world affairs.

1900

■ Eastman Kodak Company introduces the inexpensive Brownie Camera.

■ Gottlieb Daimler dies. A Daimler model is named Mercedes after the daughter of Austrian distributor Emil Jellinek.

1901

■ Britain's longest reigning monarch, Queen Victoria, dies; her son becomes King Edward VII.

The Past as Prologue

At the dawn of the 20th century, the automobile was fast becoming the major product of a mature industry. The industry's early leaders came from a variety of backgrounds: some were bicycle manufacturers, some machinists and engine builders, some involved in the carriage trade. Brilliant investors, shrewd businessmen and dynamic salesmen also played roles. Years before Walter P. Chrysler took his first job in the industry, it was populated by a range of pioneers whose names were destined to be linked to him and the Company he founded.

Among them were Colonel Albert A. Pope, Thomas Jeffrey, Charles W. Nash, Jonathan Dixon Maxwell, Hugh Chalmers, John North Willys and Roy Chapin.

Pope, the country's most successful bicycle manufacturer, was among the first to produce cars in relatively large numbers in America. Initially dedicated to electric-powered vehicles, he was by the early years of the 20th century building mostly gasoline-engine cars at his Toledo, Ohio, plant. Like Pope, the English-born Jeffrey began his American career building bicycles. Jeffrey and his son Charles constructed the single-cylinder Rambler in 1902, which became the world's second mass-

Born in Devon, England, Thomas Jeffrey immigrated to America in 1863. In 1869 in Chicago, he began manufacturing Rambler bicycles similar to those shown here. Jeffrey built his first car in 1900.

Purchasing the old Sterling Bicycle Company factory in Kenosha, Wisconsin, Thomas Jeffrey and his son Charles began producing single-cylinder automobiles in 1902, which they also called Ramblers. Shown here is the Museum's 1902 Rambler and an early advertisement for the product.

produced car after the Olds. An orphaned farm worker, Nash worked his way to the top of the Durant-Dort carriage company before following its owner, W. C. Durant, into the auto business and working his way to the presidency of first Buick, then General Motors. Maxwell, involved in the creation of one of America's earliest cars, the 1903 Haynes-Apperson, joined Ben Briscoe to found Maxwell-Briscoe, which began producing autos in 1905. Roy Chapin started out in the auto industry with Ransom Olds before joining Howard Coffin to form the Thomas-Detroit Company in 1906. In 1908, Hugh Chalmers, former vice president of National Cash Register, bought Thomas-Detroit and renamed it Chalmers-Detroit. Chapin and Coffin then launched Hudson Motor Cars, named for the Detroit department store magnate Joseph L. Hudson, who was a major investor. That same year, 1908, a salesman named John North Willys took over the foundering Overland Company. By 1917, Willys-Overland was the second largest auto company after Ford.

Over the course of the 20th century, the companies these men founded or ran would all become connected to Chrysler Corporation, most of them courtesy of the acquisitions and mergers that always played a integral role in the auto industry's dizzying evolution.

Roy Chapin, who with Howard Coffin founded the Hudson Motor Car Company in 1908, was throughout his life an active crusader for better roads and later served as Herbert Hoover's Secretary of Commerce. Shown here is a 1909 Hudson.

A Hudson maneuvers snowy lanes in an outdoor scene that might well provoke someone to champion better roads. In later years, Chapin would lead the industry switch to inexpensive closed cabs with the 1922 Essex. By 1930, 90 percent of new cars were closed models as opposed to 10 percent in 1920. Making motoring practical year round was another step in making cars indispensable transportation.

1901

■ U.S. President William McKinley is assassinated, bringing Theodore Roosevelt to the White House.

■ Ransom Olds establishes the Olds Motor Works in Detroit and begins mass production of a cheap, curved-dash Oldsmobile.

■ A massive oil strike at Spindletop, a hill outside Beaumont, Texas, sets the stage for the sharp rise in demand for gasoline-powered vehicles.

■ A new professional baseball organization, the American League, launches its first season.

1902

■ Engineer Willis Carter builds the first truly practical air conditioner.

▲ Thomas Jeffrey introduces the first Rambler, an American car featuring a single-cylinder engine and tiller steering.

■ The first Mercedes Benz Simplex is introduced.

1903

■ Edwin S. Porter produces *The Great Train Robbery*, the first feature-length film.

■ Benjamin Briscoe and Jonathan Maxwell found Maxwell-Briscoe Motor Company.

Working for the Railroad

Born April 2, 1875, in Wamego, Kansas, Walter Percy Chrysler was the son of a Civil War veteran and Kansas Pacific Railroad engineer named Henry (Hank) and his wife Anna Maria Breymann Chrysler. Walter grew up in nearby Ellis, Kansas, and upon graduating from high school in 1892 longed to become a railroad man like his father and his older brother Ed, who was serving as an apprentice machinist for the Union Pacific. Wanting at least one son to attend college, Hank refused to give his permission for Walter to enter an apprenticeship, so the

boy applied for a job as a sweeper in the railroad's machine shop. There he met master mechanic Edgar Esterbrook, who persuaded Hank to change his mind.

Beginning as a four-year apprentice, Walter soon took to the road, hopping freight trains and wandering the West, where he spent time in cities such as Cheyenne, Laramie and Rawlins, Wyoming; Ogden, Utah; and Pocatello, Idaho. Along the way, he took jobs as a mechanic with a number of railroads, including the Atchison, Topeka & Santa Fe in Wellington, Kansas, and the Colorado & Southern in Denver, before settling down in Salt Lake City with the Denver & Rio Grande

Walter Chrysler (standing at right) shows off his new 1911 Stevens-Duryea to his brother Ed.

Chrysler's boyhood home in Ellis, Kansas, is now a museum.

Walter Chrysler (right) and his brother Ed.

"I saw this Locomobile touring car; it was painted ivory white and the cushions and trim were red. . . . [O]n the running board there was a handsome tool box that my fingers itched to open."

—WALTER P. CHRYSLER

Western Railroad in 1901 and marrying his hometown sweetheart, Della Forker, to whom he had been engaged since 1897. About the time the couple had their first child, a daughter named Thelma, Walter was promoted to roundhouse foreman, supervising 90 men and earning a much-welcomed raise.

At 28, Chrysler moved his family to Trinidad, Colorado, to work once again for the Colorado & Southern, this time as general foreman. There he rose to master mechanic before moving on to the Fort Worth & Denver City Railroad in Childress, Texas, and, finally, to the Chicago Great Western in Oelwein, Iowa, where

Della gave birth to two more children, Bernice and Walter, Jr. Promoted to superintendent of motive power for the entire railroad, Walter often traveled, and on one of his many trips to Chicago, he attended the 1908 Chicago auto show. Fascinated by a $5,000 Locomobile touring car, Chrysler borrowed money through a friendly banker to buy the car and, because he did not know how to drive, had it shipped home and placed in his barn. There he took the machine apart, studying it carefully till he understood how it worked and, only then, learning to drive it. The seed of his future as an automobile industry giant had taken root.

Chrysler (eighth from left) rose from sweeping floors to master mechanic at railroads around the West as he job-hopped between companies and earned a reputation for quick, quality work.

During Chrysler's apprenticeship, he built a 28-in. working model of the locomotive his father drove.

1908

- William Durant forms General Motors.

- Charles F. Kettering forms the Dayton Engineering Laboratories Company (DELCO) to make electrical batteries for cars.

- Hugh Chalmers takes over Thomas-Detroit and renames the company Chalmers-Detroit.

1909

- John North Willys assumes control of Overland, which becomes Willys-Overland, and purchases Pope-Toledo.

- Founded by Roy Chapin and Howard Coffin, Hudson Motor Company introduces its first car, the Model 20.

- Belgian-born American chemist Leo Hendrik Baeckeland creates Bakelite, the world's first plastic.

- Alice Ramsey is the first woman to drive a car—a Maxwell—cross-country.

End of Innocence

IN 1912, WALTER P. CHRYSLER took his first job in the automobile industry heading up production at Buick Motors in Flint, Michigan; in 1915, he became president of the company. In between and half a world away, a Serbian anarchist assassinated the Archduke of Austria in the obscure Balkan capital of Sarajevo. Few Americans understood the connection between that event and their own future. In the early 1910s, most people—like Chrysler—were busy getting on with their own lives, making their careers and raising their families, when Europe burst into a war touched off by a single act of terror. Used to deferring to Europe on matters of art and culture, most Americans in general felt superior to the denizens of the Old World when it came to politics and international affairs. Americans had won handily the last war they fought with a European power, and the United States had lately strutted its new-found industrial-based might across much of the globe. Still, the country remained free of the complex network of enmities and alliances that was pulling the rest of the world apart. Feeling well out of the horror in Europe, Americans elected Woodrow Wilson president based on his promise to keep America from becoming involved in the war. But the very forces and changes that in the previous decade had made Americans so proud of their progress and optimistic about their future would ultimately drag them into the fighting. Wilson could not keep his promise, and by the time World War I ended, life in the United States had changed utterly.

When the war in Europe started in 1914, the United States was still regarded as a rural country, but when American doughboys came back from the fighting in 1919, the reality was that more of the nation's people lived in cities than on farms. Before the war, America was still a polyglot country, and immigrants were pouring onto its shores in unprecedented numbers. In the Midwest especially, one heard German spoken nearly as often as English, and foreign-language newspapers frequently served as the major source of information for millions. During the war, alien tongues were officially outlawed, immigrants were increasingly viewed with suspicion, and foreign-language papers were shuttered. By war's end, American public life had become standardized beyond anything that could have been imagined earlier.

Before the war, the flickers had been a novelty entertainment filling out the bill in vaudeville houses or viewed for a nickel by working-class men and women in the backs of city stores jerry-rigged for the occasion. The actors they saw on the silent screens had no names and were called after the seat-of-the pants production companies that made the movies: "The Biograph Girl," "The Vitagraph Girl," "The Imp Girl." By the end of the war, motion pictures were a major new industry. Films like D. W. Griffith's *Birth of a Nation* were hailed as works of art. Movies were shown on every main street in America in houses constructed solely for that purpose. And the actors not only had names but were celebrities: Charlie Chaplin, Rudolf Valentino, Fatty Arbuckle, Gloria Swanson, Mary Pickford.

In 1910, a woman's place was in the home; in 1919, she was a year away from getting the right to vote.

Airplanes, which previously had been a wonder-causing novelty, now were a major new weapon of war, used to bomb cities and civilians. Before the war, a man could still buy a drink on his way home from work; by 1919, there wasn't a bar left open in the entire country, and folks could go to jail for purchasing bathtub gin from the local bootlegger. In 1910, a few people, most of them living in cities, owned cars, while even fewer farmers drove Model Ts. By 1919, cities were choked with traffic, and teens across the country were driving their family flivvers to town on Saturday night.

World War I did not cause all these changes. The movies took off after William Fox went to court in 1911 to break up Thomas Edison's Motion Picture Trust and after Carl Lammele first promised to make Pickford a "star" in order to steal her from Biograph. Prohibition and women's suffrage had been making their way up the Progressive political agenda since the late 19th century. Henry Ford transformed the automobile into the nation's major durable good when he created the modern assembly line in 1913. And in many ways, these developments had more of an impact on American life than the Great War. The movies, far more than the war, helped break down main-street culture. Prohibition for the first time fed huge amounts of cash into the hands of urban gangs and helped turn them into an organized underworld. Cheap automobiles put Americans on the road to tourist destinations and family vacations. When Ford offered his workers $5 a day to build his car, a riot broke out among job seekers thronging his Dearborn plant the next day. This was only the first hint of the revolution he was creating in the working world—in consumer habits and in the everyday notion of prosperity—that historians would compare to the 1917 Bolshevik upheaval in Russia.

The war did, however, accelerate many of these changes. The hard-drinking German and Irish immigrants who filled American cities and formed the main bulwark of the opposition to Prohibition before the war were silenced by the patriotic fervor accompanying it. New car manufacturers like the Dodge Brothers, already successful at selling Americans good quality, inexpensive cars, got a huge boost from Army orders for trucks and cars. The war produced flying aces, who—calling themselves daredevils—barnstormed the

On location in the Hollywood hills, the bespectacled director Marshall Neilan poses Mary Pickford in front of his cameras for a scene in the movie M'liss.

country with postwar stunt shows that made them heroes and the idea of flight commonplace. The Creel Committee, which produced anti-German propaganda during the war, fed its personnel and techniques into the ever more sophisticated postwar American advertising business, which in turn helped to create growing consumer demands. Farm boys who went into the war having never eaten in a restaurant or attended anything more sophisticated than a church social, came back from Europe smoking cigarettes and wearing wrist watches and trench coats and harboring new ambitions and needs.

Concerned that these soldiers, instantly discharged after the war, might flood the streets of the nation's cities, Army officials insisted that each soldier be interviewed by the Red Cross or the YMCA, indoctrinated against the evils of urban life and urged to leave for home immediately. The railroads were induced to offer a discount of two cents per mile to any soldier who would buy a ticket for home within 24 hours of discharge. Some did, and a few of those brought back to communities around the country the deadly influenza virus they had picked up Over There, causing an epidemic that claimed millions, including the Dodge brothers, as its victims. Polio, virtually unheard of in America before the war, also followed the doughboys home. Others did not return home but began looking for new jobs where they could use the skills they had learned in the Army. The mechanics among them flocked to new airplane manufacturers springing up around the country and to the makers

of automobiles, increasingly centered in Detroit.

Just as they were arriving, Walter Chrysler was leaving the business. Having made Buick a major success and in the process become a very rich man, he retired in 1919. As he left, the industry that had been so boosted by wartime sales and inflated wartime prices found itself hard hit by an inventory depression created by the end of the war. Even General Motors and Ford were in trouble, and companies like Willys-Overland that had once competed effectively with the two giants tottered on the edge of bankruptcy. With a strange new ambition of his own—to build a new car for a new generation with his name on it—Chrysler returned and accepted the challenge of pulling the ailing Willys-Overland back from the brink.

Trucks and ambulances mobilize in support of the American Meuse-Argonne offensive in 1918.

Dodge Tough

The Dodge brothers, John and Horace, trained as machinists in their father's Port Huron, Michigan, shop before joining the Murphy Engine Company in Detroit in 1886. After working at the Dominion Typograph Company in Windsor, Ontario, Horace invented a dirt-resistant bearing in 1896. In typical fashion, he shared credit with his brother and together with Fred Evans formed the Evans & Dodge Bicycle Company. When the Canadian Cycle & Motor Company bought E & D in 1901, the Dodges moved to Detroit to establish a machine shop—soon to be the largest in the city—where they built transmissions for the Olds Motor Works. In 1903, Henry Ford offered them shares in the Ford Motor Company if they would retool to build Ford engines, transmissions, axles, brakes, frames and steering gears. The first Fords were made entirely by Dodge except for the wheels, tires and a wooden box of a body. The brothers gave up all other business, paid for retooling expenses and devoted their entire shop to the Ford account.

The arrangement proved mutually profitable and made Ford and the Dodges millionaires. But as Ford threatened to make more of his own parts, the brothers

Although both John and Horace Dodge died in 1920 from the effects of influenza, the company continued into the decade retaining its reputation for the production of inexpensive but well-made automobiles. When Walter P. Chrysler negotiated the purchase of the company in 1928, he considered its reputation and the goodwill it enjoyed with the public to be among many Dodge assets.

At their Hamtramck plant, the Dodge brothers were known for personally testing their products. John drove two Dodge prototypes into a brick wall at 15 to 20 mph and was rumored to have chosen U.S. Chain Tread tires for Dodge products after dropping various tires off a four-story building and watching them bounce.

felt pressure to cut costs. Ford failed to renew some contracts that expired in 1912 and 1913, and when the Dodges offered to sell their interest in his company back to him, Ford rejected their terms. The brothers then decided to build their own car, designed by Horace, at their modern plant in Hamtramck, Michigan. Launched in 1914, Dodge Brothers benefited from John and Horace's established reputation for quality, and they received more than 22,000 applications for dealerships. By 1916, Dodge production was the nation's fourth largest.

The following year, the brothers sued Henry Ford and won, forcing the Ford Motor Company to distribute profits rather than plowing them back into the business. An angry Ford bought out all minority stockholders, making the Dodges, with a 10 percent interest, $25 million richer. Dodge Brothers' domestic sales were enhanced with U.S. Army contracts to supply cars and trucks in 1916 for General John Pershing's expedition in Mexico and, beginning in 1917, for the Allied effort in Europe. Even after their deaths only months apart in 1920, the brothers retained a stellar reputation as two of the most ingenious, dynamic and competent men in the titan age of the automobile industry. Chrysler bought Dodge Brothers in 1928.

1914

■ The first vehicle bearing the Dodge Brothers name is a four-door touring car dubbed "Old Betsy."

■ Henry Ford announces a $5 per day wage and an eight-hour work day, sparking a riot among job seekers at the Highland Park plant.

■ The assassination of Austria's Archduke Ferdinand and his wife in Sarajevo sparks the Great War in Europe.

▼ Jonathan Maxwell reorganizes Maxwell-Briscoe into Maxwell Motors, the only firm to emerge from defunct United Motors.

The 1915
Dodge touring car.

In 1916, General John Pershing's young lieutenant George S. Patton, Jr., used three Dodge touring cars in what may have been the first "mechanized charge" in military history. Afterward, the general was so taken with the automobile's rugged reliability he notified the U.S. War Department that in future he wanted only Dodges for use in the Mexican campaign. In all, the Army bought 250 touring cars for service in the Mexican Badlands, two of which are shown here.

1915

■ A German U-boat sinks the Lusitania, adding to the increasing cry for war in the traditionally isolationist United States.

■ German aircraft maker Hugo Junkers builds the first all-metal airplane.

The Miracle Worker

In 1911, after a dispute with the president of the Chicago Great Western, Walter P. Chrysler walked off his job as the company's superintendent of motive power and took his first steps toward a new career in automobiles. Out of work with a family to support, he called on an old acquaintance, Waldo H. Marshall, president of the American Locomotive Company in Pittsburgh, and applied for a job with the locomotive builder. Hired as superintendent of the company's ailing Allegheny plant, Chrysler was promoted to works manager as he turned an unprofitable factory into an efficiently run, money-making operation. His newly acquired reputation as a plant "doctor" got him noticed by one of ALCO's directors, James Storrow, who happened also to be chairman of General Motors' Finance Committee. When Storrow suggested he go see Charles Nash, president of Buick, Chrysler jumped at the chance to join a major player in the burgeoning new auto industry. He took a job as works manager at Buick even though it meant a big reduction in salary.

Pausing just long enough for Della to give birth to the Chryslers' youngest, Jack, Chrysler moved his family from Pittsburgh to Flint, Michigan. There again he raised

Chrysler, his reputation as a company "savior" growing, stands with other corporate notables of the day.

H.Firestone   J.Rosenwald   Thomas Edison   Sir Thomas Lipton   Chas.Schwab   Henry Ford   W.P.Chrysler   Geo.Eastman   T.A.Wilson

Walter Chrysler sits (front, third from left) with workers from Buick Motor Company in Flint, Michigan.

production, improved efficiency, lowered costs and increased profits, persuading the famously frugal Nash to increase his pay, first from $6,000 to $25,000, then to $50,000. In 1912, Nash became president of General Motors, but GM founder William Durant regained control of the company by merging it with Chevrolet. When Nash made plans to leave in 1915, Durant made Chrysler an offer he couldn't refuse—the presidency of Buick and $500,000 annually (three-fourths of it in GM stock). Chrysler's contract lasted three years, and so did he. He and Durant clashed constantly, and in 1919, at age 45, Chrysler retired. The next year, Willys-Overland's credi-

tors asked Chrysler to reorganize the severely troubled company, once the world's second largest automaker after Ford. Della, having had her fill of her husband and his cronies hanging around the house, willingly packed for the move to company headquarters in New York. The creditors were taken aback by Chrysler's demand for $1 million a year but accepted his terms. Cutting costs, trimming salaries, tightening business practices and personally dealing with suppliers and creditors, Chrysler slashed the debt and saved the company and thereby greatly enhanced his already considerable reputation as a corporate "miracle worker."

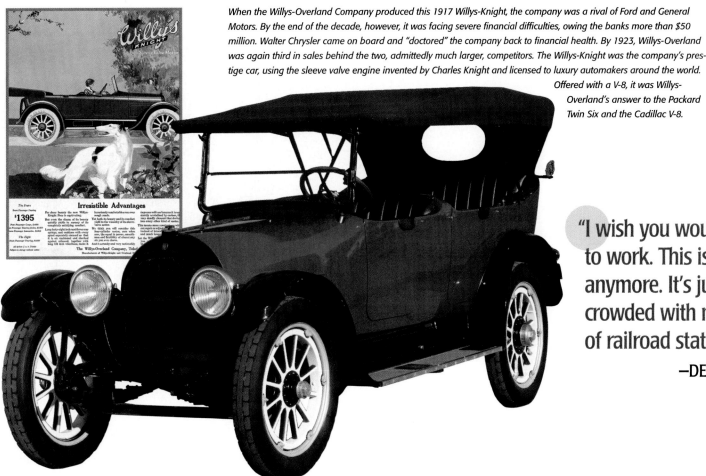

When the Willys-Overland Company produced this 1917 Willys-Knight, the company was a rival of Ford and General Motors. By the end of the decade, however, it was facing severe financial difficulties, owing the banks more than $50 million. Walter Chrysler came on board and "doctored" the company back to financial health. By 1923, Willys-Overland was again third in sales behind the two, admittedly much larger, competitors. The Willys-Knight was the company's prestige car, using the sleeve valve engine invented by Charles Knight and licensed to luxury automakers around the world. Offered with a V-8, it was Willys-Overland's answer to the Packard Twin Six and the Cadillac V-8.

> "I wish you would go back to work. This isn't a home anymore. It's just a place crowded with men. A sort of railroad station."
>
> —DELLA CHRYSLER

1918

■ The first Nash appears, Model 681, powered by an overhead valve six-cylinder engine.

■ The fighting comes to an end in Europe with the Armistice on November 11.

■ An influenza epidemic breaks out in Europe as soldiers return home from Indo-China and quickly spreads round the world.

1919

▲ Ratified by three-fourths of the United States, the 18th Amendment becomes law, banning the manufacture, sale or transportation of liquor and launching the country into the Prohibition era.

▼ The "Black Sox" scandal rocks the nation when New York and Boston gangsters bribe eight members of the Chicago White Sox into throwing the World Series to the Cincinnati Reds.

■ The Treaty of Versailles, formally ending World War I, is concluded.

The Making of the Jazz Age

IN 1920, THE U.S. CENSUS made it official: for the first time more Americans lived in cities than on farms. As a result, the Roaring Twenties became the decade when the metropolis fired the modern imagination and dominated contemporary culture.

Assembly-line mass production, which had made the American auto industry so successful, had become part of the fabric of economic and social change, and its effects were ubiquitous, cumulative and often subtle. For the first time, workers made enough money to buy the products they produced, and automakers counted on their purchases to fuel industry growth. That growth, in turn, fed the unification of the nation through a network of roads. The Good Roads Movement, spearheaded by Hudson's Roy Chapin, had become gospel for automakers, and the 1920s would witness the opening of the first paved national road, the Lincoln Highway. All this helped to foster a consumer-driven society—people drove to stores to buy goods delivered over long distances and stopped along the way to eat and amuse themselves. World War I had accelerated the spread of assembly-line production techniques to other industries, and factories of all kinds in the North's industrial regions offered decent paying semiskilled or unskilled jobs to the country's poorest.

Just as Detroit's assembly lines were stoking American industry and Ford's Model Ts were transforming small town life, the industry's first mass-produced tractors were also having a wide-ranging impact on American agriculture. By 1918, the new tractors were allowing American farmers to meet the soaring demands of war-torn Europe as former farm boys were shipped off to fight. By 1922, land once reserved for animal feed could now grow crops, and for the first time crop surpluses became normal. Surpluses brought low prices, but farmers could not cut production since they needed to sell everything they grew to pay for the new equipment. Family farms went bankrupt; corporate agribusinesses bought up the farms on which the banks foreclosed. As tenant farming and sharecropping spread among whites, black tenant farmers and share-croppers were forced out of the fields that required ever fewer hands to bring in a crop. These displaced farmhands, rendered unnecessary by mechanization, poured into the segregated neighborhoods of the North's urban centers—New York's Harlem, Chicago's South Side—by the millions. It was no accident that the Harlem Renaissance occurred in the 1920s, nor that New York, Chicago and Kansas City became centers for the blues and for jazz.

The jazz the black musicians played had about it a whiff of the forbidden, not simply because it transgressed racial boundaries, but also because the venues where they—and many of the white bands who took up the music—performed belonged to the underworld of illegal booze and big city vice. For the decade of the 1920s was also the era of Prohibition. From January 1920 to April 1933, the federal government forbade the manufacture, transport and sale of alcoholic beverages anywhere in the United States under the Volstead Act, passed to provide for enforcement of the recently ratified 18th Amendment. The moment the act went into

THE NEW
112 H.P. CHRYSLER
IMPERIAL "80"

Justly the
Choice of those
Who Know the
Finest

Every day the new 112 h.p. Chrysler Imperial "80" is winning new allegiances—
winning new owners from among motorists familiar with the best of other cars.

Because, by every test by which automobiles are judged, it is superior to these other
cars in performance, quality and value.

Not alone because it is one of the world's most powerful motor cars, but because
that power is translated into terms of flawless performance.

Not alone because its bodies are remarkable for their long graceful lines, their fine
upholstery and fittings, their charm and diversity of chromatic coloring. But because
in these hand-built bodies by Chrysler, Locke, LeBaron and Dietrich, is that well-
defined note of restraint that speaks true smartness.

For performance with superlative comfort and the individuality of exclusive bodies,
this splendidly-engineered and precision-built Chrysler is justly the choice of those who
know the finest motor cars. Hence, the swing to the new 112 h. p. Imperial "80."

Roadster (with rumble
seat), $2795; Five-Pas-
senger Sedan, $2945;
Town Sedan, $2995;
Seven-Passenger Sedan,
$3075; Sedan-Limou-
sine, $3495; also in
custom-built types by
Dietrich, Le Baron and
Locke. All prices f. o. b.
Detroit, subject to current
Federal excise tax.

In this advertisement for the Imperial, Chrysler sells the glamorous new lifestyle of the 1920s along with its automobile.

effect, America became a nation of lawbreakers.

In the big city ethnic neighborhoods, inhabited by the very same immigrants who filled the Detroit factories at Rouge River and Hamtramck, neighborhood bootleggers began immediately to brew bathtub gin, abetted by local grocers, who supplied the necessary raw materials, and by former saloon keepers, restaurant owners and ice cream parlor operators, who helped distribute the product. Lured by the promise of easy profits, the gangland underworld moved in on these mom-and-pop operations. Rival gangs, their members often no more than teenagers, battled each other for control of "territory," making liberal use of sawed-off shotguns and Thompson submachine guns, which were available cheaply and in quantity as U.S. government surplus from the recent war, to establish their local monopolies and far-flung trucking empires. The mobsters worked hand in glove with local political machines, securing votes and furnishing graft in return for protection from police interference. They poured their profits into networks of illicit bars, saloons and nightclubs, and in these speakeasies jazz played over the machine-gun tattoo in the background. The most ambitious realized that meeting the demand for illegal alcohol effectively would require a degree of organization hitherto unheard of in criminal activity, and the deals struck in the mean streets of the city percolated up the power structure until much of the country's political administration and law enforcement had been corrupted.

Even baseball had fallen under the influence of New York and Boston gangsters when they bribed eight members of the Chicago White Sox to throw the World Series of 1919 to Cincinnati. The connection between the national pastime and organized crime threatened to end professional baseball forever. The timely appointment of Judge Kenesaw Mountain Landis as commissioner helped save the game. Enforcing strict regulations on players, Landis also approved the use of a livelier baseball with a new cork and rubber core, which dramatically increased the frequency of crowd-pleasing home runs and paved the way for the almost mindless adulation baseball fans would heap on the young George Herman "Babe" Ruth, whom the New York Yankees signed for $125,000 in 1920.

Ruth's accomplishments in the 1920s were the stuff of baseball legend, but the fact that Americans considered him a genuine hero had something to do with a game that celebrated individual achievement and excellence in a time when the factory system and mass production had imparted the stamp of anonymity to most objects of human creation. Ruth and a number of other sports stars playing on every kind of field were the beneficiaries of a cult of celebrity that was part of the 1920's café society and consumer culture. Fed by the motion picture industry, the cult deified such "stars" as Charlie Chaplin and Mary Pickford, who, along with the sports heroes, led lives endlessly fascinating to their fans. Professional gossip, for all intents invented by Walter Winchell, became a standard feature of both local and national news in the 1920s. And, although he started with a gossip column in the tabloids, Winchell achieved the pinnacle of his influence through the new broadcast medium of radio.

On November 2, 1920, radio station KDKA in Pittsburgh broadcast the results of the presidential election. Within three years, there were 556 commercial radio stations in the United States. On-air advertising, at first perceived as an invasion of privacy and greeted with widespread objection, was "indirect"— singing groups, comedians and bands adopted a company's name without ever mentioning a product's merit, price or point of purchase. Despite these obstacles, advertisers were quickly drawn to the new networks—the National Broadcasting Company (NBC), the Columbia Broadcasting System (CBS) and the Mutual Broadcasting System (MBS)—which had forged a national audience. To this audience Winchell reported the comings and goings of celebrities galore in the cafés and nightclubs of New York. And through these radio networks the siren call of the saxophone beckoned the young in the back parlors and the small town cafés to jump in their roadsters and head for a movie house or dance hall—or a speakeasy—in the city.

Once they got there, many never went back.

This new audience also had a major impact on the way the automobile industry subsequently developed. For one thing, growth of a huge urban middle class fueled the continued expansion of automobile production. To sustain that expansion, the industry created immensely powerful advertising departments to push their products on the radio and in slick new magazines—*Town and Country, Smart Set, New Yorker,* even *Time*—that sprang into existence to serve as the middle-class window on the good life of a consumer culture. Not only did café society's cult of celebrity ensure that the automakers employed the famous in every field to endorse their products, but automobiles themselves became a measure of success and celebrity. Al Capone was as famous for his steel-plated bulletproof Cadillac as he was for his scarred face, and when President Herbert Hoover tried to come up with a phrase to fix the goal of American prosperity, he hit upon the promise of "two chickens in every pot, and a car in every garage."

In the 1920s, the watchwords of society for everything from household goods to high art became "make it new," and the new urbanites, rich and tipsy, were fascinated by both the stylish and the sinful. The times were right for General Motors' new head, Alfred P. Sloan, to introduce "planned obsolescence"—minor stylistic alterations for each year's models and a major overhaul every three years as a psychological ploy to enhance sales. The times were less friendly to Henry Ford's dowdy Model T, favorite of farm folk everywhere, whose production was suspended. The times welcomed the closed cabs that Roy Chapin championed with his popular Essex. And it was in these new times that Walter P. Chrysler introduced an automobile bearing his own name, with a revolutionary six-cylinder engine that made the smooth ride and easy handling formerly associated only with luxury models commonplace. Aficionados would call it the first "modern" car—and "modern" was precisely how people in these times wanted to feel.

- The 1920 U.S. Census documents that, for the first time, more Americans live in cities than on farms.

- Pittsburgh's KDKA reports the results of the presidential election in the first commercial radio broadcast.

- ▲ The 19th Amendment to the U.S. Constitution is ratified, giving women the right to vote.

- The U.S. Congress rejects the Treaty of Versailles, which had called for a League of Nations opposed by American isolationists.

- U.S. Attorney General A. Mitchell Palmer, using a list of "alien radicals" prepared by a young J. Edgar Hoover, jails or deports thousands of immigrants in the "Red Scare."

- Alfred P. Sloan, the new head of General Motors, introduces "planned obsolescence."

The Birth of a Company

In 1920, the Maxwell Motor Company, like its larger competitors, was suffering from an economic downturn in the auto industry. To reverse its fortunes, Maxwell hired Walter P. Chrysler, who had earned a reputation as a corporate "doctor" when he the came out of retirement the year before to save the ailing Willys-Overland. Once a middle of the pack producer of some 40,000 cars annually, Maxwell had seen its output fall to 6,000 cars per year in 1921 and its once solid reputation become frayed because of shoddy engineering. As the chairman of

Maxwell's reorganization committee, Chrysler quickly raised fresh capital, reorganized the company's production and beefed up the frail rear axle that had led to most of the customer complaints. He dubbed the reworked cars The New Good Maxwell and mounted an advertising campaign to unload the inventory. He next ordered production of a new model, Model 25, and by 1922, production rose to 55,000 cars.

Chrysler also brought with him the three talented engineers—Fred M. Zeder, Owen R. Skelton and Carl Breer—he had met at Willys-Overland. As Chrysler continued his revitalization of the Maxwell, the team of engi-

On May 7, 1921, the Maxwell Motor Corporation was formed by combining the old Maxwell Motor Company with the Chalmers Motor Car Company. Three years later, the corporation dropped the Chalmers line entirely, but production of Maxwells continued at the plant at Jefferson Street and Outer Belt Line.

Walter P. Chrysler was a man who understood the automobile business. His work at Buick, his success in reducing debt at Willys-Overland and his resuscitating the Maxwell Motor Company gave him the experience as well as the drive to start his own auto company in 1925.

When Walter P. Chrysler took over as the head of the ailing Maxwell Motor Company in 1920, he faced an operation that was losing money and a stockpile of about 26,000 Maxwell cars. The public spurned the Maxwell because of problems caused by its weak rear axles and faulty gas tank mounts. Chrysler sent mechanics out to repair each of the 26,000 cars. Mounting a marketing campaign to reassure the public of the Maxwell's quality, he offered The New Good Maxwell. The public was impressed, the cars sold at a profit ($5 per car), and Walter Chrysler turned the Maxwell company around.

neers (whom he soon began calling the "Three Musketeers") designed in 1922 a new vehicle that the "Boss" approved before seeing the prototype. The trio tested their new car—boasting engineering firsts, advanced mechanical features and a rakish new design— only after dark along Detroit's Kercheval Avenue, and the public did not see the automobile until January 1924 at the New York Auto Show where a new marque, "Chrysler," was born.

Although Walter Chrysler loved to tell a story about his being denied space to display the new marque at the New York Auto Show in January 1924, the February 1924 issue of *Motor Vehicle Monthly* ran pictures of the new car and described it in detail among the 74 makes of cars present at the show. The magazine noted that the "new Chrysler cars were distinctive and, being low, produced an impression of length." The car was an immediate success, not only with the exhibitors and potential investors passing through the lobby, but also with the public. Chrysler came away from New York with a promise from a Chase Security banker to underwrite $5 million in corporate bonds and a plan for the future. In 1925, the Maxwell Motor Company was rechristened the Chrysler Corporation.

The first car to bear the Chrysler name appeared before the American public in early 1924, while Walter P. Chrysler still served as the head of the Maxwell Motor Company. Available in six body styles, the new Chrysler boasted a high-compression, 201 cu. in. inline L-head six-cylinder engine and four-wheel Lockheed hydraulic brakes. In the first year of production, about 20,000 Chryslers were sold. Here, Chrysler proudly displays the first car to bear his name, this one, a two-door brougham.

"I remember saying, I would not touch [the Maxwell] with a ten foot pole…what I would not touch was later on revealed to be the greatest opportunity of my life."

—WALTER P. CHRYSLER

The Chrysler logo first appeared on the new 1924 cars and has remained over the years an assurance of quality and value.

1920

▲ The New York Yankees sign George Herman "Babe" Ruth for $125,000, launching a golden age in baseball.

■ Both Dodge brothers die.

■ Willys-Overland hires Walter P. Chrysler to reverse the company's declining fortunes.

1921

▲ Walter P. Chrysler is brought in to rescue the ailing Maxwell Motors and launches a brilliant advertising campaign to sell his mechanically improved version of the company's car, The Good Maxwell.

■ The Federal Highway Act directs the Bureau of Public Roads to pursue an "adequate and connected system of highways."

- Benito Mussolini leads a march on Rome to become dictator of Italy and Europe's first Fascist leader.

- British archaeologist Howard Carter and his patron, Lord Carnarvon, open the tomb of Egyptian pharaoh Tutankhamen ("King Tut") to make the richest discovery in the history of archaeology.

- Ferdinand Porsche becomes Daimler's chief engineer and designer and introduces the "S" series cars.

- Insulin is used for the first time to treat diabetes.

- The first car radio is introduced.

▼ Hudson introduces the Essex sedan, which at only $300 more than a touring car, leads the shift, over the rest of the decade, to cars with enclosed passenger cabins.

A New Kind of Stop and Go

In the mid-1920s, the new Chrysler Corporation was regarded as one of the stronger independent car companies, ranked in the same breath with Hudson, Packard, Nash and Studebaker. The original Chrysler lineup had consisted of six body styles designed to fit Walter P. Chrysler's notion that the public had a desire for, as he put it, "a real quality light car—one not extravagantly large and heavy for one or two people, but adequately roomy for five, economical to own and operate." Since 1920, the automobile industry had been operating under the new strategy, first developed by General Motors' Alfred P. Sloan, of planned obsolescence—the introduction of minor stylistic alterations for each year's models with major overhauls, in which several improvements were batched, every three years. Like the other automobile companies, Chrysler worked toward continuous improvement—changing its body styles, introducing new models and even launching new marques to broaden its market. All the more important, then, was Chrysler's innovative engineering, which often produced "firsts" that became industry standards and established the Company's reputation for mechanical excellence.

For Maxwell Motors' last production years, Walter P. Chrysler approved the installation of a hydraulic braking system in its Chalmers cars. Asked by Chrysler to test the new feature, Fred Zeder, Owen Skelton and Carl Breer found it not at all reliable. Breer completely redesigned the system and installed it on the first Chrysler Six. Hydraulic brakes required less pressure and fewer finicky adjustments than the rods and levers of mechanical brakes. The first to offer such brakes on a moderately priced automobile, Chrysler made sure customers knew it. Below is a schematic of the system from Chrysler's 1924 product literature.

Walter P. Chrysler (far left) met the three talented engineers—(left to right) Carl Breer, Fred Zeder and Owen Skelton—while he was helping to resuscitate the fortunes of Willys-Overland and brought them with him when he took over at Maxwell Motor Company. There the first car the Three Musketeers designed for him proved a hit with the public, helped launch the Chrysler marque and boasted the kind of engineering excellence that would become a hallmark of their long tenure at Chrysler Corporation, where they remained a force until 1950.

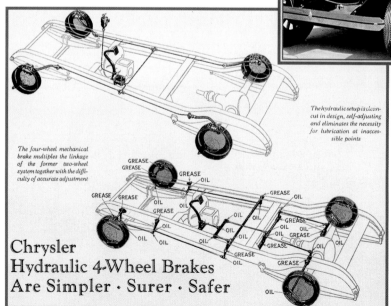

The hydraulic setup is icon-cut in design, self-adjusting and eliminates the necessity for lubrication at inaccessible points

The four-wheel mechanical brake multiples the linkage of the former two-wheel system together with the difficulty of accurate adjustment

Chrysler Hydraulic 4-Wheel Brakes Are Simpler · Surer · Safer

> "Selling the public on four-wheel hydraulic brakes was a rough go. The only hydraulic brakes used on automobiles were on Duesenberg which was five times higher priced."
>
> —CARL BREER

The innovation began with the very first Chrysler and was born of the combined genius of three engineers—Fred M. Zeder, Owen R. Skelton and Carl Breer. The 1924 Chrysler that attracted such attention at the New York Auto Show came with one of the notable engines of the decade—a light, powerful, high-compression six-cylinder that matched in performance the power plants in some of America's most expensive cars. Its increased efficiency—offering more power for a given amount of fuel—and smoother operation were economy features. So was the replaceable oil filter that went with it, which—because it ensured the circulation of clean oil—protected engine bearings and reduced the number of oil changes the car needed. By the late 1920s, except in the lowest end of the market where four-cylinder engines continued to hold sway, six- and eight-cylinder high-compression engines mimicking the landmark Zeder-Skelton-Breer Six were the rule, and some sixes even broke the $1,000 price barrier. By the late 1930s, another feature of the original Chrysler, four-wheel hydraulic brakes providing smoother straighter stops, were commonplace throughout the industry.

1922

■ Chalmers merges with Maxwell Motor Company.

■ The Harlem Renaissance, the most important movement in African American literary and visual art, begins with the publication of poet Claude McKay's *Harlem Shadows*.

1923

■ Dodge becomes the first automaker to use an all-steel body for a "closed body" auto.

■ Henry Luce launches *Time* magazine.

■ Nitrocellulose paint is introduced, dramatically shortening the time it takes to paint a car.

The new Chryslers, like this 1924 touring car, boasted a number of mechanical and engineering firsts. While the soft-top touring cars were not to last long in the Chrysler lineup, two of the innovations—high-compression six-cylinder engines and four-wheel hydraulic brakes—were destined to become standard not only in Chryslers but in automobiles throughout the industry.

The most notable engine of the 1920s was the high-compression six-cylinder. Based on research that Sir Henry Ricardo had conducted into "turbulent head" design, the engine Zeder, Skelton and Breer created used a turbulent head configuration that reduced engine knock. The valve-in-block engine head design, combined with a seven-bearing crankshaft, developed 68 hp at 3,000 rpm.

▲ Ford's Model T prices hit an all-time low of under $300 (without a self-starter). This same year, the company's 10-millionth Tin Lizzie rolls off the line.

■ In the Teapot Dome oil leasing scandal, a federal jury indicts former Interior Secretary Albert B. Fall, oil executive Harry Sinclair and Edward L. Doheny for bribery and conspiracy to defraud the United States.

■ Franklin Delano Roosevelt contracts polio, a disease rare in the United States before World War I.

▼ Congress passes the Johnson-Reed Act, which effectively slams the door on further mass immigration into the United States.

United We Stand

In January 1920, John and Horace Dodge attended the National Auto Show in New York City where both men fell victim to the influenza epidemic then sweeping the country. John died in New York on January 14 after his flu developed into full-blown pneumonia. Weakened by illness and emotionally devastated by John's death, Horace succumbed the following December. In January 1921, Frederick Haynes, who had been with the brothers since their bicycle days, became president and general manager of Dodge. Haynes steered the company through economic hard times until 1924, when John and Horace's heirs decided to sell the business. After they rejected an offer by General Motors' Alfred P. Sloan, the company was run briefly by three Detroit businessmen—Joseph, Robert and Ray Graham—before the New York banking firm of Dillon, Read & Company bought Dodge Brothers for $146 million. Haynes left over differences with Clarence Dillon, who had dreams of merging Dodge with Packard, Hudson and the Briggs Body Company, and company Chairman Edward Wilmer took over as president. Dillon's merger plans came a cropper, Dodge sales began slipping, and the banking firm's enthusiasm for

"Buying Dodge was one of the soundest acts of my life. I say sincerely that nothing we have done for the organization compares with that transaction."

—WALTER P. CHRYSLER

The year Walter P. Chrysler took over Dodge, the company was producing this popular two-toned Senior Six sedan.

the automobile business soon soured in the face of growing debt. In 1928, Dillon turned to Chrysler as a potential—and safe—investor. The negotiations attracted national attention because the acquisition of Dodge Brothers could well vault Chrysler Corporation into the top ranks of the industry alongside GM and Ford.

Chrysler and Dillon met in a suite at the Ritz-Carlton Hotel in New York for five days of intensive, round-the-clock bargaining before the deal was finally struck. In exchange for Chrysler stock valued in the market at $70 million and the assumption of some $56 million in Dodge debentures, the Company got Dodge's established dealerships and sales force and its excellent production facilities—including an iron factory and modern forge shop—along with its "Dependability Car" reputation for making cheap and reliable products. Late on the afternoon of July 31, 1928—mere hours after the deal was closed—big signs that read "Chrysler Corporation, Dodge Division" adorned the Dodge facilities in Detroit just as the nation's evening newspapers hit the streets proclaiming the merger, the biggest in the automobile industry's 32-year history. "Rarely in any industry at any time," wrote *Fortune* magazine a little later, "does a late starter… drive so quickly into a commanding position."

During the years immediately following the deaths of the Dodge brothers, the automobile industry was beset by an economic recession. As sales plummeted and profits were squeezed, two types of vehicles helped bolster the company—closed cars and trucks. After Walter Chrysler took over, although he introduced design changes and new marques, he also continued to produce the durable trucks, such as this 1929 Dodge pickup, that had long been a company standard.

The negotiations between Dillon, Read & Company and Walter P. Chrysler for the takeover of Dodge Brothers were no secret and, in fact, attracted much attention both within the auto industry and on Wall Street. Once the deal was struck, it made headlines around the country.

1924

■ Thomas Watson founds a company named International Business Machines, or IBM.

▲ A new marque is born as Maxwell Motors produces the first Chrysler Six, with engineers Zeder, Skelton and Breer's innovative high-compression engine and four-wheel hydraulic brakes.

1925

■ Chrysler Corporation is incorporated on June 6 in Delaware. Chrysler Canada is launched.

■ The last Maxwell rolls off the line.

■ General Motors hires Harley Earl to "style" the LaSalle.

▼ The Lincoln Highway, America's first paved national highway, opens.

- The first *New Yorker,* an imitation of H. L. Mencken's *Smart Set,* is published for "caviar sophisticates."

- Balloon tires become standard in the automobile industry.

- ▲ F. Scott Fitzgerald publishes *The Great Gatsby,* a novel that becomes a classic of the Jazz Age.

- The Florida land boom peaks as speculation in property surpasses any other business stampede in U.S. history.

- ▲ The Ku Klux Klan, reborn the year before in the Midwest, holds a huge rally in Washington, D.C.

- The first international Art Deco Exposition is held in Paris.

- Dayton, Tennessee, high school teacher John T. Scopes is arrested for teaching Darwin's theory of evolution, which leads to the famous "Monkey Trial."

New Additions to the Family

About the time Chrysler acquired Dodge Brothers, the Company introduced two new marques to the American automobile world—DeSoto and Plymouth—thus expanding its market and positioning the Company to compete with General Motors. Plymouth represented the lowest-priced of the Company's offerings, Dodge offered mid-priced cars, and Chrysler went after the higher end of the market. DeSoto, targeted at GM's Oakland and Pontiac buyers, was introduced in a price range below Dodge. Both Plymouth and DeSoto were in the works before

Walter P. Chrysler sealed the Dodge deal, and many believed he was seeking Dodge's manufacturing capabilities and dealers more than the brand name.

The fanfare had begun on April 23, 1928, when Dow Jones Services carried a news item announcing the formation of DeSoto Motor Corporation as a division of Chrysler and its intention to build the DeSoto Six, "which is non-competitive with any of the other four Chrysler lines." The DeSoto nameplate already announced, Chrysler continued with his plans despite Dodge dealer worries that he meant to kill the Dodge line. Rolling off the assembly line at Highland Park, the

Chrysler's entry into the low-priced market with cars such as this 1928 Plymouth coupe not only allowed the Company to weather the economic hard times ahead but also helped establish its reputation for well-engineered, distinguished cars regardless of price. The Plymouth offered many engineering features unique to its price range, such as hydraulic brakes, oil filter and pressure lubricator, and was also enhanced by a slender-profile radiator, bowl-shaped headlamps, crowned fenders and a high-compression Silver Dome engine. By 1930, Plymouth franchises had been given to all Chrysler, Dodge and DeSoto dealers.

DeSoto made its public debut on August 4, 1928. By year's end, nearly 35,000 cars had been shipped, and the dealer force had grown to 1,500, recruited mostly from Dodge dealerships. After 12 months of operation, the DeSoto Division had produced 80,000 cars, including this 1929 DeSoto roadster— a remarkable first-year record for any automobile manufacturer in any price range. Fourteen months after the division was organized in March 1928, with Chrysler Vice President Joseph E. Fields as its president, the Corporation shipped its 100,000th DeSoto.

1929 model-year lineup included a roadster, phaeton, business coupe, deluxe coupe, two-door coach, four-door sedan and four-door deluxe sedan, all priced under $1,000, from $845 to $955. Distinguishing DeSotos from other cars in the same price range were features such as Lockheed four-wheel brakes, Delco-Remy ignition, rubber engine mounts and Lovejoy shock absorbers, all standard.

Plymouths were even cheaper. Introduced as a 1928 model, the Plymouth Model Q replaced the four-cylinder Chrysler 52, which had succeeded the Maxwell Model 25-C. The first low-priced car to offer features such as four-wheel hydraulic brakes, full-pressure engine lubrication instead of the splash system, lightweight aluminum-alloy pistons, a hand brake independent of the service brakes and an optional oil filter, the Plymouth was priced between $670 and $725. Until Chrysler could complete the new Lynch Road plant, the cars were assembled at the Highland Park facility. By May 1929, the Company was turning out some 1,000 Plymouths a day. As *Time* magazine noted, Chrysler had "gone into the low-priced field with the throttle wide open." It was indeed a timely expansion for Chrysler, in large measure enabling the Company to survive the Great Depression.

Chrysler's two new marques were introduced with typical aggressiveness. Although the first Plymouth rolled off the assembly line amid great secrecy on June 11, 1928, the first public showing came a month later, on July 7, when famed aviator Amelia Earhart drove one of the cars onto a stage at Madison Square Garden in New York City. A little later, 300,000 people crowded into Chicago's Coliseum to see the Plymouth, as dealers across the country dressed like Pilgrims to promote the new car. Both Plymouth and DeSoto found their sales boosted by Chrysler's marketing staff, whose ad purchases made the Company's offerings overall the second most advertised vehicle line in the United States. By decade's end, Chrysler was third place in sales.

At the Track

Once word of the high performing new Chrysler Six reached those in the motor sports world, stripped-down racing versions began showing up in competition. Ralph de Palma, who had driven the Six in the 1924 Mt. Wilson Hill Climb in record time and who had covered 1,000 miles in the car in 786 minutes on a board track in California, was the first to race the

Model B-70 in the United States. Five months later, another Six debuted at Le Mans, France.

Walter P. Chrysler himself was a fan of the 24-hour road race at Le Mans, and long before many American automobile companies even considered entering the event, Chryslers had garnered respect at the French race. In 1925, a pair of Chrysler Sixes, entered independently, made the race. One, driven by two Frenchmen named Henry Stoffel and Lucien Desvaux,

Ralph de Palma, racing trophy in hand, stands by his Chrysler Six.

failed by two laps to travel the miles needed to complete the race, but the second—one of the many Chrysler "white machines" to come—not only finished the necessary 177 laps but came in seventh overall.

A consortium of Chrysler enthusiasts sent a team of four Chrysler 72s to Le Mans in 1928. The 24 hours soon devolved into a fight between a team of Bentleys, highly favored, a Stutz, and two of the Chryslers. For a time it appeared that one of the two Chryslers—driven by Stoffel and André Rossignol and the Ghica brothers—might pull off a victory for Walter P.'s creations. Instead, the "Bentley Boys" and the Stutz came in first and second, while the Chryslers finished a distant third and fourth. Still, third and fourth place was a remarkable showing at the six-year-old event—which was already becoming well known and was destined to become an endurance classic—and erased any doubts about the new marque's reliability and durability.

Independent racers entered the Six, shown below, at Le Mans in 1925, where it raced against much more expensive cars. The Six would also post amazing results at the Hours of Spa and Mille Miglia races.

The team of Chryslers racing in the 1928 Le Mans endurance classic line up for a photograph. The upstart cars came close to stealing the race from the favored "Bentley Boys" team but ultimately came in third and fourth behind a Bentley and a Stutz.

"[The Chrysler Six racer was] a 70 mph car when 50 mph was considered fast, and a mile a minute was probably considered reckless."

—RAY JONES AND MARTIN SWIG, *CHRYSLER IN COMPETITION*

1928

- George Eastman exhibits the first color motion pictures in Rochester, New York.

- Sir Alexander Fleming discovers penicillin, the first "wonder" drug.

▲ Louis Armstrong releases *West End Blues*, the first fully realized recording of classic American Jazz.

- Chrysler Export division is organized.

1929

- Architect Mies van der Rohe inaugurates the no-frills International Style at the 1929 International Exposition in Barcelona, Spain.

- Ferdinand Porsche resigns and is succeeded by Hans Nibel as chief engineer and designer at Mercedes-Benz.

▼ The New York stock market crashes, heralding the Great Depression.

The Dark Valley

ON OCTOBER 29, 1929, the bottom fell out of the American stock market. "Black Tuesday" was the worst single day in the history of the New York Stock Exchange, and thousands of Americans lost everything they owned. But the stock market crash was less the cause than the harbinger of the dark valley of economic and political despair into which the nation and the world was about to plunge for most of a decade.

Financial panics and industrial crises had long been familiar to capitalist economies like that of the United States. But American production had soared in the last three decades due to technological advances, the introduction of mass assembly techniques and infusions of money into new industries. All these put the latest collapse on a scale beyond the imagining of those in government and banking whose business it was to tend the free market system. By 1930, consumers simply could not afford to buy the cornucopia of new goods industry was producing; companies cut back production; workers lost their jobs; markets for new goods shrank or disappeared altogether; banks failed; credit dried up; and money all but ceased to flow into the economy. Not knowing what to do about this unprecedented severe downturn in the business cycle, President Herbert Hoover refused to call it either a panic or a crisis. America, he said, was experiencing a "depression," which sounded decidedly less ominous to him.

But the term took hold, and the era became known as the Great Depression. During that era, nearly a third of the American work force became unemployed. Hungry millions stood in lines in every city and town in the country for bread, soup and what little public and private relief was available. In the Midwest, a combination of years of overproduction and severe drought denuded much of the nation's farmland and created massive dust storms that darkened the sky at noon. As banks foreclosed on farms, former farmhands and sharecroppers piled their wives and children and their few worldly belongings into the family jalopy and took to rutted roads heading west out of the great Dust Bowl and on to California. Elsewhere, when families lost their homes, they moved to disease-infested slums with dwellings constructed of packing crates and scrap metal, which they called, with grim humor, "Hoovervilles." In 1932, 20,000 out-of-work World War I veterans descended on Washington, D.C., demanding the bonuses they had been promised for their service to their country but which Congress refused to pay now. Hoover sent federal troops under the command of Douglas MacArthur to the Anacostia Flats, where the veterans had set up camp, to clear out the "Bonus Army" with bayonets, tear gas and tanks.

Like all segments of the economy, the automobile industry felt the impact of the Great Depression. Bank failures reached a climax in 1932, creating a credit crisis that severely damaged an industry whose market depended almost entirely on credit purchasing. Rather than buy new models on time, car owners suddenly seemed to realize that their automobiles were indeed durable goods and hung on to them instead of trading them in. For the industry as a whole, produc-

Bread lines such as this one were a daily sight in the Great Depression.

Overland, Packard and Studebaker. Gone were such prestigious names as Pierce Arrow, Auburn, Cord, Franklin, Stutz and Peerless. Billy Durant's dream of creating a second auto empire with Durant Autos perished in 1932. The Big Three—Ford, GM and Chrysler—also survived, though not unscathed. Ford, at first doing well with its relatively cheap Model A, slipped to third place before the decade was over. In 1932, GM posted a profit of just $165,000 compared to $248.3 million in 1929, selling only 5,810 cars during the month of October, about the average daily sale in 1929. Cadillac was saved as a make only by a decision to extend credit to the black professional class. But Chrysler, though it lost money one year, actually gained market share.

By all odds, Chrysler Corporation should have been severely crippled by the Depression. Walter P. Chrysler had come to the game late. He was still trying to restore loyalty to a company that had suffered a decline in the years between the death of the Dodge brothers and his takeover, and he had just introduced two new marques—Plymouth and DeSoto—when the bottom fell out of the market. Yet the new cars (especially the Plymouth), excellently engineered, boasting many innovations and selling at a reasonable price, proved exactly the right product for such hard times. By 1933, production of the Plymouth had reached a quarter million, and even the disastrous sales of the new and radically innovative Airflows could not prevent the Corporation from assuming second place in the industry.

Despite some damage, the automobile business in general recovered from the sales slump of the Great Depression more quickly than other sectors. Once the models people had bought early in the decade truly

tion fell 37 percent in 1930 and another 30 percent in 1931. Employment was down two-thirds from 1929, and payrolls dropped to half what they had been as companies cut wages, shortened the work week and instituted periodic shut downs. By 1932, auto production was less than 25 percent of its pre-Depression high, GM and Nash alone among automakers made a profit, and Nash outearned GM.

Independent automakers were the hardest hit, and by mid-decade 30-odd small and struggling companies had dwindled to a mere handful, the so-called Little Five—Nash-Kelvinator, Hudson, Willys-

began to wear out, middle-class Americans resumed buying new cars even if it required sacrifices elsewhere. By 1934, they were trickling back into show rooms across the country. In other ways, however, the Depression continued to affect developments in Detroit.

In 1932, Franklin Delano Roosevelt was elected president promising a New Deal for Americans. Under his administration, labor unions for the first time experienced real support from a federal government traditionally hostile toward working-class organizations and their activities. In 1935, John L. Lewis, the fiery United Mine Workers' president, founded the Committee for Industrial Organizations, which soon broke with the American Federation of Labor (AFL) to become a much more radical association. The Congress of Industrial Organizations (CIO) believed in organizing unions by industry rather than by craft or trade, and one of the first and most powerful new unions was the United Auto Workers of America. In the mid-1930s, the UAW staged a series of strikes for recognition of the union at GM and Chrysler. The industry vigorously resisted these efforts. When Ford tried to disrupt organizing efforts at its Rouge River plant with paid thugs and strong-arm tactics, a violent and bloody battle broke out. With the New Deal government as midwife and mediator, however, the UAW soon became an established player in the industry.

By the time Walter Chrysler retired in 1935, a brave new world was stirring—and not just in the automobile business. The Great Depression was a worldwide event, and it had fostered changes across the globe that were gaining a dangerous momentum. In Europe and Asia, the economic crisis had helped usher in a new kind of political order: fascism. By the mid-1930s, the major fascist powers—Japan, Italy and Germany—had begun campaigns of conquest that would lead directly to another world war. World War II would do what the New Deal ultimately could not—end the Great Depression and return America to its full industrial strength. It had taken Chrysler just a decade—half of which was spent in the debilitating economic crisis of the Depression—to win and hold his Company's ranking as one of the Big Three. Now that Company would play a significant role in the coming war and the heyday of the U.S. auto industry that followed.

Ford Motor Company's strong-arm squad approaches union organizers (from left) Robert Kanter, Walter Reuther, Richard Frankensteen and J.D. Kennedy shortly before the Battle of the Overpass at its Rouge River plant on May 26, 1937.

▲ Gandhi begins the civil
disobedience movement
in India, agitating for
independence from
Great Britain.

■ Astronomers discover a
new planet: Pluto.

■ Karl Benz and Wilhelm
Maybach die.

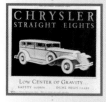

▲ All mid-range auto companies begin equipping their
cars with eight-cylinder
engines: the first Hudson,
Nash, Dodge and DeSoto
Straight-Eights appear.
(Chrysler Eights are introduced the following year.)

■ Walter Chrysler completes
New York's Chrysler
Building as a private
venture.

The Three Musketeers

By the 1930s, the three talented engineers Walter P. Chrysler first met at Willys-Overland—Fred Zeder, Owen Skelton and Carl Breer—had become the heart of Chrysler Corporation. At Chrysler, it was the powerful Engineering Department that dominated the direction of the Company, and it was the Three Musketeers who dominated the Engineering Department.

Born the son of a blacksmith in Los Angeles on November 8, 1883, Breer parlayed an early interest in steam cars—which he designed, built, demonstrated and serviced—into a degree in mechanical engineering from Stanford University in 1904. After graduation, he went to work for the Allis-Chalmers Manufacturing Company near Milwaukee. There he met and befriended Fred Zeder. In 1911, Breer returned to Los Angeles, where he worked in truck manufacturing, started and sold a service and accessory business and opened an experimental garage and auto shop. In 1916, Zeder, who was chief engineer at Studebaker Brothers in South Bend, Indiana, invited Breer to come help organize an engineering research division.

Born on February 9, 1886, in Edgerton, Ohio,

In the mid-1930s, the power and prestige of the Three Musketeers at Chrysler became evident when they created a startling, new, aerodynamically designed automobile. The Airflow failed commercially, but its design and innovations had a widespread influence throughout the industry. This Airflow publicity shot features (left to right) Zeder, Chrysler and Breer; other publicity photographs included Skelton as well.

Skelton worked from 1905 to 1907 at the Pope-Toledo plant, which was known for its advanced engineering. Leaving Toledo for the design drafting department of Packard Motor Car Company where he specialized in transmissions, Skelton ultimately hooked up with Zeder at Studebaker in 1914. There, his design experience with rear axles, drives and gear boxes helped expedite the creation of a new Studebaker line debuting in 1918. By that time, Skelton, Breer and Zeder had formed a working partnership that would eventually take them to Chrysler.

The creator of that team, Fred Zeder was born on March 19, 1886, in Bay City, Michigan, and graduated from the University of Michigan with a B.S. in mechanical engineering in 1909. After completing his apprenticeship at Allis-Chalmers, Zeder took charge of the laboratory at the Everett-Metzger-Flanders Company in 1910. When Studebaker took over EMF in 1913, Zeder became a consulting engineer for the corporation, then—a year later—its chief engineer. By 1916, Zeder had gathered to his side both Skelton and Breer just as the company reached a peak in production and then began a decline to the brink of receivership. The team, meanwhile, stayed together, and ultimately made engineering history at Chrysler.

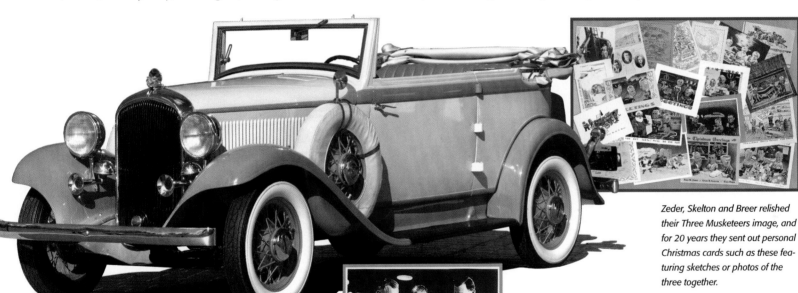

In the 1920s, with the creation of the Chrysler Six high-compression engine, the Three Musketeers had initiated or made commercially feasible any number of innovations that during the 1930s became standard on all makes of automobiles: high-compression engines, hydraulic brakes, Floating Power (a new way of mounting engines to reduce vibration), downdraft carburetors, air cleaners, oil filters, one-piece curved windshields and many others. In the early 1930s, two of these—downdraft carburetors and Floating Power—were touted on new-model Plymouths, such as the 1932 convertible above.

Zeder, Skelton and Breer relished their Three Musketeers image, and for 20 years they sent out personal Christmas cards such as these featuring sketches or photos of the three together.

Zeder, Breer and Skelton

Chrysler was so known for its innovations and engineering excellence that Zeder, Skelton and Breer themselves became a selling point for the Company, as evidenced in this advertisement featuring the Three Musketeers.

▲ Franklin Delano Roosevelt, newly elected the 32nd president, announces a "New Deal" for Americans.

■ Work begins on the Golden Gate Bridge in San Francisco.

■ Dodge begins using the Ram hood ornament.

■ Plymouth reaches the number three spot in automobile production.

■ Ford introduces a V-8— Henry Ford's last triumph.

■ Hugh Chalmers dies.

▲ Only two automakers— General Motors and Nash— turn a profit, with Nash outearning GM.

- The 18th Amendment is repealed, and Prohibition comes to an end.

- Walter P. Chrysler allows John North Willys to use "Floating Power" in the Willys Model 77, the car that saves the company from bankruptcy; Willys-Knight is discontinued.

▲ Adolf Hitler becomes chancellor of Germany.

- Vladimir Zworkyn, director of electronic research at RCA, conducts the first television broadcast, over a radio wave relay between New York and Philadelphia.

- The Essex is renamed the Essex Terraplane. Equipped with a Hudson Eight, it achieves sensational performance and speed records.

- The first Chrysler-engineered Dodge trucks appear.

Known for the New

Always innovative, Chrysler engineering by the 1930s boasted a string of "firsts" that set the standard for automobile production and became a selling point for all Chrysler models.

The year 1930 saw the introduction of the downdraft carburetor. Inherently more efficient than the updraft design then universal on passenger models, downdraft carburetors had been used on racing cars for years. Zeder, Skelton and Breer adapted the available technology to introduce downdraft carburetors on cars coming off the regular production line. The next year, Chrysler announced Floating Power. Early automobiles suffered from the effects of inherent engine imbalance and strong torque pulses. These vibrations were felt and heard by passengers and were especially objectionable during hard acceleration and in four-cylinder vehicles. Chrysler engineers realized that redesigning and relocating the engine mounts could achieve a substantial reduction in these problems.

Floating Power was an unusual feature on an inexpensive car. Chrysler's advertising took full advantage of this fact, selling Plymouths for two decades with the

The downdraft carburetor, a major breakthrough in engine design, was a feature on this 1931 Imperial dual cowl phaeton. Old updraft carburetors were typically mounted low on the side of the engine. Downdraft carburetors, mounted above and to the side of engines, used both suction and gravity to pull in a cooler air and fuel mixture. The intake system had less restricted passages, making for better low-end torque, more horsepower, a more efficient fuel mixture and easier starting.

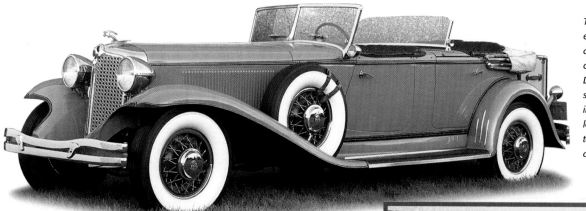

In 1931, Plymouth vehicles incorporated an industry first—Floating Power. By using carefully designed and much softer rubber mounts located so that the center of gravity of the engine and transmission mass was on its natural rotational axis, Chrysler's engineers relieved much of the discomfort passengers felt in earlier cars. In this illustration from a 1930's ad, at upper left, is the traditional four-point suspension; at upper right, the center-line engine mounts of Floating Power. The engine mountings at lower left lie below the engine's center of gravity. At lower right, the center of gravity is on the center line of rotation.

claim that they had the smooth ride of an eight-cylinder engine but the economy of a four.

Many of Chrysler's innovations in the Great Depression of the 1930s were aimed at more economical production. The Company pared the engine lineup to the necessary minimum and designed many engines to be machined on the same line, sharing pistons, rings, wrist pins and other basic components. Chrysler also developed a new means of finishing surfaces and machined parts that reduced friction wear and extended their useful life. Calling the process "Superfinish," the Company used the durability of its product,

as well as engineering advances, to sell its cars.

The most startling innovation of the decade, the aerodynamic design of the Airflow, was not a success with the public. Buyers found other features more intriguing, such as the automatic overdrive transmission and a new kind of ignition, which started the car when the driver turned a key and depressed the accelerator pedal rather than pushed a button on the dash. Chrysler used these innovations to raise the expectations of consumers, who increasingly looked for greater sophistication in the industry's products, even as many cars grew cheaper to buy.

1934

■ The first of three years of widespread and severe drought, which will help create an agricultural "Dust Bowl," strikes the American West.

■ Chrysler's sales surpass Ford's, making Chrysler Corporation number two in the industry.

■ Chrysler introduces Airflow design on its Chrysler and DeSoto models.

■ Chrysler sets up the Airtemp air-conditioning and heating division.

■ Ray Dietrich becomes Chrysler's chief stylist.

■ Joseph Stalin launches the first of a series of sweeping and deadly purges of the Soviet Union's Communist government.

▼ The first drive-in theater opens.

■ The Essex part of the Terraplane name is dropped.

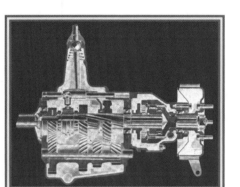

Introduced on some 1933 models, the All-Helical-Geared Transmission (top right) ensured "silent second speed and positive easy shifts" through gear teeth cut at an angle to the gear shaft, instead of parallel. The new spiral design greatly reduced gear noise, because the gear teeth meshed gradually. In 1939, Chrysler's engineers took the next significant step with the development of Fluid Drive. Essentially an input fan and an output windmill operating in a sealed chamber full of oil, this innovation allowed the engine to idle in gear with the car standing still, and the vehicle could be accelerated—slowly—without using a clutch. In addition, the vehicle could be driven in high gear and then automatically shifted into overdrive, providing a semiautomatic transmission. The driver had to use the clutch to shift into high gear. The clutch was also necessary to shift into reverse or the lower gears.

By the time the 1939 Dodge coupe at right came off the line, Chrysler had introduced a number of innovations to economize in production. Many engines shared the same basic design and could be produced on the same line using many of the same parts. Most significantly for consumers, Chrysler's Superfinish created parts surfaces so fine that Company engineers came up with the term "micro-inches" to measure their irregularities. This type of machining reduced friction and increased the life of parts.

■ John Maynard Keynes
publishes *The General
Theory of Employment,
Interest and Money*, introducing a new economics
of monetary policy and
deficit spending.

■ Pan-American Airways
begins trans-Pacific service
from California.

▲ Walter P. Chrysler resigns
as head of Chrysler
Corporation to be suc-
ceeded by K. T. Keller.

■ United Mine Workers'
leader John L. Lewis organ-
izes a committee of industrial unions that breaks
away from the American
Federation of Labor (AFL)
to become the more mili-
tant Congress of Industrial
Organizations (CIO).

■ John North Willys dies.

The Thoroughly Modern Airflow

In 1934, Chrysler Corporation introduced a radically new streamlined design for what has been called "the first modern automobile." The brainchild of engineer Carl Breer, the Airflow was a milestone in Chrysler history. Although its design features were widely copied in the years after its introduction, the car proved a failure with the buying public for reasons still debated by automobile historians and Company aficionados.

Emerging from a series of unrelated compromises, the typical automobile body of the late 1920s was essentially a big box for people behind a little box for the motor. Breer, with his associates Fred Zeder and Owen Skelton, believed that the high-compression engines they had developed for Chrysler simply could not realize their potential using such ungainly bodies. Early tests indicated that cars met less wind resistance driving in reverse than moving forward. The Three Musketeers began to wonder if some of the principles used in aircraft design might help in streamlining cars. They consulted with aviation pioneer Orville Wright, who

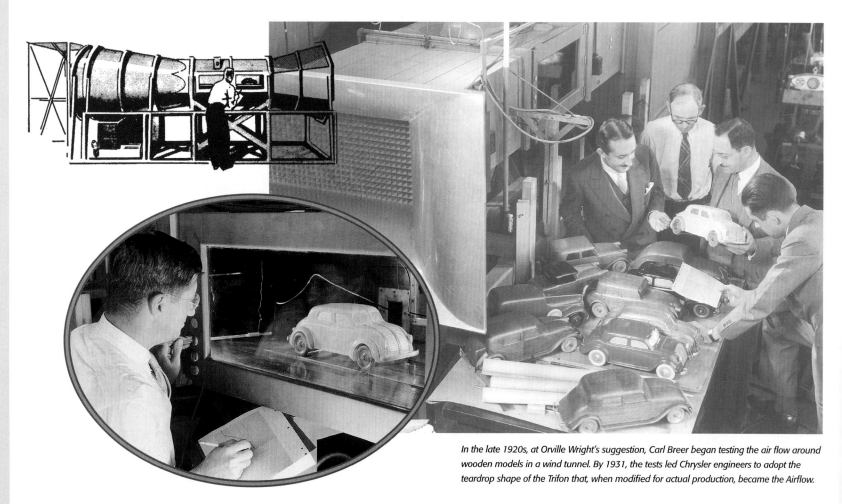

In the late 1920s, at Orville Wright's suggestion, Carl Breer began testing the air flow around wooden models in a wind tunnel. By 1931, the tests led Chrysler engineers to adopt the teardrop shape of the Trifon that, when modified for actual production, became the Airflow.

suggested setting up a small wind tunnel to test the resistance of a series of wooden scale models. Walter Chrysler had a larger tunnel built at Chrysler's Highland Park headquarters so that Zeder, Skelton and Breer, learning aerodynamics as they went along, could carry on their investigations. They were hoping to find a form that might employ air "lift" in reverse and press the new car more firmly against the road at high speeds. A first for the industry, the wind tunnel tests continued into 1931 and led to the development of a modified teardrop shape for the new design. A

number of running models later, the engineers had come up with the Trifon Special, which was later dubbed the Airflow.

Impressed by the Airflow test model's smooth ride and ample interior space, Walter Chrysler gave the engineers the go-ahead without much thought about the car's unconventional design or the danger of launching a radically different product in hard economic times. The Company had a good backlog of orders early in 1934, but summer sales proved dismal. DeSoto, wholly committed to Airflow design, saw sales

What most fascinated the public about this 1934 Chrysler Airflow—apart from its looks—was probably its overdrive transmission, which would automatically engage in second and third gears when the driver accelerated to 45 mph and lifted his or her foot from the accelerator pedal. The car became best known, however, for its radical design. Like a section of an airplane wing, it rose in a parabolic curve from the front bumper and trailed off to the rear. This teardrop form was stepped to accommodate the sloping and divided windshield, which could be opened from the bottom. The shape was reinforced by the slight upturn and thinning of the trailing edges of the fenders. The fenders and the headlamps were absorbed in the single rising curve of the front facade. Much of the ornamentation, inside and out, was self-consciously Art Deco, a style at the time associated with streamlining and modernity.

▲ Eugene O'Neill becomes the first, and so far the only, American dramatist to win the Nobel Prize for literature.

■ Gordon Buehrig designs the Cord, still considered by many the most beautiful car ever created.

▲ Mercedes-Benz debuts a diesel-powered car, the 260.

■ German troops, unopposed, occupy the demilitarized Rhineland.

■ Nash buys Kelvinator to secure its president, George W. Mason, who succeeds Charles Nash.

■ Walter Chrysler personally recruits the industry's first woman to serve as an automotive engineer, M. Virginia Sink.

1936

- The Olympic Games are held in Berlin, and African American athlete Jesse Owens steals the show with four gold medals.

- The New Deal federal government completes Boulder Dam (renamed Hoover Dam in 1947), the biggest dam in the world and the largest public works project in modern history.

- The Spanish Civil War, precursor to World War II, begins.

- Dodge revives the convertible sedan.

- Hit by hard times, Dust Bowl families migrate by car to California where they are dubbed "Okies."

1937

▲ Organizing into the United Automobile Workers of America, laborers at Chrysler and General Motors stage the first "sit-down" strikes in the country's history.

DRAWING ROOM *Luxury* . . .

A new sense and appreciation of what luxury really is, is immediately apparent upon inspection of these superb new interiors . . . yet in the design of every detail maximum utility has been given full consideration along with comfort. Seats as wide and as deeply cushioned as divans—doors as wide as those in your home—there is ample leg room for complete relaxation—a luggage compartment behind the rear seat back—a carrying space in the rear compartment of the business coupe equal to that of a dray and a host of other interior refinements and advantages made possible by Airflow design. Features such as these should have your careful consideration before making the purchase of any motor car.

The Airflow's engine lay 20 in. farther forward than normal, reaching past the front axle. Passengers sat within the car's wheelbase, nearer the middle of the car, on seats that stretched 50 in. across. Fifty-five percent of the car's weight was borne on the front tires (as opposed to about 40 percent in other autos of the period), which—though it gave the Airflow its odd nose—enabled Chrysler to use more closely matching springs, front and back. All of these changes improved the Airflow's ride, especially in the back seat, contrasting sharply with the rocking and pitching of all but the heaviest of its contemporaries. In this ad, Chrysler emphasized the advantages this new design offered for the interior of the car.

When sales proved disappointing, Chrysler tried to make the Airflow more acceptable to the buying public mainly by modifying its grille to change the strange-looking rounded front of the car. From left to right are one of the two original 1934 grille designs and new designs for 1935, 1936 and 1937.

slip 47 percent below those of the previous year, and Chrysler held on to its market position only because the Company also offered an array of more traditional and much cheaper Airstream models. Chrysler brought in a team of stylists who—unable to do much about the basic shape of the car—gave it a series of face lifts with ever more conventional grilles and head-lamps. Meanwhile, plans for Airflow versions of Dodge and Plymouth were quickly dropped. The failure of the Airflow, while not disastrous for the Company, which actually lost money only in 1934, shook Chrysler's confidence. In the coming decades, the Company, once renowned for its innovations, became decidedly less adventurous.

1937

■ Despite the New Deal, the U.S. sees a new decline in economic conditions.

■ Frank Whittle builds the first jet engine.

■ Japan goes to war with China.

■ Hudson's Terraplane is phased out.

1938

▲ *The War of the Worlds*, a broadcast radio adaptation of H. G. Wells' novel about an invasion from Mars narrated by Orson Welles, ignites a major panic among listeners.

■ In the *Anshluss*, Germany occupies and annexes Austria.

★ *Airflow* IMPERIAL CHASSIS AND FRAME

Airflow design has made it possible to provide the most rigid chassis and frame ever built. . . . Notice the steel girders surrounding and protecting the occupants and absorbing shocks. In actual construction many of the body frame members shown above are integral with the body panels—the one reinforcing the other.

The Airflow pioneered unit-body construction by producing a well-integrated body and stressed-steel frame. Although the Airflow's body was not yet completely of a unit with the chassis, its construction did make for a lighter and stronger car, which Chrysler demonstrated in a publicity stunt typical of the time. After tumbling down a 100-ft. cliff in Pennsylvania, an Airflow then drove away under its own power.

- Wallace H. Carothers patents nylon for the Du Pont Company.

- Walter P. Chrysler falls ill and retires from the Company's chairmanship. Mrs. Chrysler dies.

- The U.S. Army issues a call for the development of a light reconnaissance vehicle to replace the motorcycle-and-sidecars then in common use.

- Robert Cadwallader replaces Ray Dietrich as Chrysler's head stylist.

- At the Munich conference, Great Britain appeases Adolf Hitler by agreeing to his occupation of the Sudetenland, a region of Czechoslovakia.

Training Ground

The establishment of the Chrysler Institute of Engineering was a measure of the importance Chrysler Corporation afforded its Engineering Department. General Motors President Alfred P. Sloan's doctrine held that GM should not seek to be an engineering leader, but instead to keep pace with the industry. Henry Ford remained committed to his "universal car." In contrast, Walter P. Chrysler, emphasizing innovation and engineering excellence over styling and repetition, reasoned that if you built better cars, people would buy them.

Thus, in the early years, Chrysler Corporation always had a proportionately larger engineering work force than its competitors, and its engineering approach was spread throughout the Company.

By 1928, the Corporation's talented Three Musketeers, Fred Zeder, Owen Skelton and Carl Breer, supervised more than 500 engineers. They had discovered that when they hired men from the competition, they spent a year retraining them. Hiring inexperienced engineers proved even more time-consuming. They set up an apprentice system to bring graduate students from various universities into the Corporation.

In addition to the two-year course for university graduates, the Institute offered shop men a high-school and technical education through night courses. Chartered by the State of Michigan to issue high-school credits, the Institute awarded fellowships to selected shop men who attended universities of their choice. By the late 1930s, the program had a waiting list of about 5,000.

Founded in 1931, the Chrysler Institute of Engineering was incorporated and, in 1933, authorized by the State of Michigan to confer engineering degrees up to and including a master's in automotive engineering. It was the only industry-related school in the country at that time to offer such degrees. The Institute's basic purpose, besides shortening the course necessary to train engineers and draftsmen, was to bring university research and science laboratory equipment and experience into the arena of the manufacturing process itself.

The Institute set a quota of students from each of the best scientific schools in the United States and abroad. Visiting representatives from the Institute conducted personal interviews to choose the cream of each year's technically educated crop. Thirty to 50 graduates of scientific universities and institutions were accepted annually into the two-year course. Rather than paying tuition, those who qualified received salaries, the equivalent of endowed scholarships from the Institute. By bringing together the latest in laboratory facilities, hand-picked candidates, specially directed training and top-notch instrumentation, the Institute helped launch a new era in automobile engineering.

During the students' second year at the Institute, most work assignments took place in the laboratory, where students rotated from department to department every few months. In this 1940's publicity photo for the Institute, students look on as an instructor lectures on the workings of a Chrysler engine.

The Institute soon opened its own building in Highland Park. The course of study began with lectures by the top technical men in Chrysler's Engineering Department. The rest of the first year was broken into quarterly units: experimental garage, a three-month stint in one of Chrysler's production plants under the wing of a resident engineer, a quarter in Engineering's drafting department and a final quarter in the engineering and research departments of the production divisions.

When Zeder, Skelton and Breer looked for someone to head the Institute, they discovered John Caton working in Chrysler's Dodge plant. Formerly a professor directing the automotive engineering department of the University of Detroit, Caton had taken a leave of absence to gain experience on the line, and the Three Musketeers—according to Breer—found him in overalls inspecting a Dodge truck. Shown here is the first Chrysler-engineered truck, the 1933 Dodge pickup. Chrysler made these service vehicles, always a mainstay of Dodge, the epitome of the Company's approach to automaking.

- John Steinbeck publishes *The Grapes of Wrath*.

- Paul Muller invents DDT.

- In August, Adolf Hitler and Joseph Stalin sign a non-aggression pact, which clears the way for a German invasion of Poland.

- In September, without a formal declaration of war, Nazi Germany invades Poland, commencing World War II.

- Willys-Overland develops concept drawings in response to the U.S. Army's call for a light reconnaissance vehicle, the first step toward the creation of the Jeep®.

- *Gone with the Wind* premieres in Atlanta.

A Global Conflict

On December 7, 1941, Japan launched a surprise air attack on the American fleet anchored at Pearl Harbor, Hawaii. From the Japanese standpoint, the attack was inevitable. It led to the United States going to war not just with Japan but also with Europe's fascist powers, which President Franklin Delano Roosevelt saw as equally inevitable. The war that began for America that sleepy Sunday morning—the 20th century's second worldwide conflict—would be the great, central, cataclysmic event of the age. And it changed everything.

When Japan struck, the United States was already preparing for war. It was openly providing supplies and equipment to the European Allies, who had been fighting since 1939. Armaments were pouring out of the country's factories. The year before, Congress had passed the first peacetime draft in the nation's history, and the armed forces were rapidly expanding. For months, the government had been waging an undeclared war against Germany in the Atlantic. And yet, the American public remained deeply divided over the drift of U.S. policy toward declared war. The surprise attack ended the debate, and a united America entered the war. Congress granted the president unprecedented powers to wage global war, and Roosevelt used them with grim determination to complete the mobilization of the nation.

The automobile industry contributed mightily to the war effort. The Office of Production and Management (OPM), headed by General Motors President William Knudsen and labor leader Stanley Hillman, had been the centerpiece of Roosevelt's program for peacetime mobilization. Though compliance was voluntary and OPM lacked a clear-cut policy (Knudson would perform far more effectively as a production troubleshooter in the War Department after the fighting started), it nevertheless laid important groundwork in such areas as retooling and new plant capacity. When war suddenly arrived, these—along with Detroit's production and management know-how, its strong credit lines and its effective lobbying—made the automobile corporations the obvious choice for major defense orders. Certainly most Americans after Pearl Harbor looked to Detroit to furnish the tools of war. Fifteen days following the attack, *Time* magazine summed it up: "The U.S. need only step on the gas." Cost-plus government contracts guaranteed large profits without risks, and given such sure-fire incentive American big business, led by the auto industry, worked a production miracle that astonished the nation, its allies and its foes.

First and most quickly came the production of trucks and other military vehicles, while the more challenging retooling was underway to employ automotive production technology in the building of complex aircraft and aircraft engines. Some companies used existing facilities; others threw up entirely new plants—such as the huge Dodge factory near Chicago built to the produce B-29 Superfortress engines. Everything imaginable was adapted to the assembly line. In a former cornfield outside Detroit, Chrysler operated a massive factory with a line a third of a mile long from which

Glenn Miller and his band
entertain the troops.

Swedes took 450 man-hours to build was churned out by relatively unskilled Americans in 10 hours. And then there was the Jeep®, a case study of the role of big business in the arsenal of America, which Willys-Overland turned into a symbol of the war.

The impact of the war extended far beyond Detroit. The day after Pearl Harbor, thousands of Americans rushed to enlist, and the U.S. government conscripted millions more. Boys hardly old enough to drive a car, much less vote, would soon be dropping bombs on centuries-old centers of Western culture or dodging bullets in some of the most godforsaken spots on earth. Quickly trained, hastily assigned enlisted personnel were expected to repair, supply and operate the most sophisticated machinery produced by the modern world under impossible conditions ruled by a complex bureaucratic apparatus that regulated their every hour and their very fate. Whether they carried out routine duties behind enemy lines or endured the most extreme conditions of heavy combat, they fought boredom, isolation, loneliness, homesickness and debilitating fear. They contracted exotic diseases, manned bleak outposts and ran short of supplies in the middle of deserts, surrounded by jungles, on tiny islands and amid the rubble of war-torn civilizations. Living in drafty Nissen huts, dank caves and moldy tents and eating food they detested, they strove to find ways to pass the time when they weren't fighting the enemy. They gambled and drank to excess, read old magazines, comic books and paperback novels, watched sappy movies, listened to Frank Sinatra and Glenn Miller on the radio when they could get them, Tokyo Rose and Lord Haw Haw when they couldn't, took weekend passes and attended USO shows. Mostly they lived for mail call and longed for home.

rolled Sherman tanks. Before Detroit got hold of the Swedish-designed Bofors—the finest rapid-fire anti-aircraft weapons in the world—they were expensive and limited by extensive hand-crafting. Chrysler engineers completely revamped Bofors manufacture into a step-by-step mass-production mode, and a gun that the

Back home, those Americans who did not march off to war found themselves caught up in the conflict as well, since World War II touched almost every aspect of American life. The government regulated automobile tires, cars, shoes, farm machines, gasoline, sugar and meat, among hundreds of other commodities. It established a point system, allowing only 50 points per month for canned goods when a can of tomatoes cost 20 points. Almost no one could afford steak or pork chops, and butchers offered unrationed shark meat at 45 cents a pound. All over the country, in vacant lots and backyards, Americans planted Victory Gardens to supplement their diets. Since the government had set a 35-mph speed limit to conserve gas and tires, highway patriots honked their horns at speeders—three short blasts and a long one, Morse code for "V." Salesmen joined car pools. Women went to work in factories and found the resulting economic freedom exhilarating. Grandparents volunteered for Civilian Defense. Farmers found themselves short of labor, because not only had many farmhands volunteered or been drafted, but thousands had left for well-paying and draft-exempt jobs in the war plants. For the rich and some of those paid in the inflated wages of the big cities, black markets sprang up in everything from nylons to new tires.

Sixteen million Americans went to war. They, and the world they lived in, were transformed by the holocaust. The level of destruction in Europe and Japan was almost unimaginable. The Nazi death camps and the nuclear annihilation of Hiroshima and Nagasaki cast a somber shadow over the future. But the war had revived the Depression-hobbled industrial might of the United States, promising a prosperity unimaginable before the war. Despite these changes, however, in

In the small print of this ad, Chrysler takes note of its wartime production. In fact, production of 1942 models for private sale ended early in the year.

1945 the stuff of dreams for most Americans remained humble enough: a house of their own, an education for them and their kids, a new car, a set of good tires and a world without gas rationing. And many of them had the money to make such dreams come true. Fat wartime payrolls had produced a huge jump in personal income—$172 million, an increase of 68 percent over 1939. This, along with the American production capability that had been so expanded by war, meant the pump was primed. The good life, the one for which Americans had fought and sacrificed over the last four years, was just around the corner.

■ Richard Wright publishes *Native Son*, an eloquent and violent, but vivid and persuasive depiction of the African American experience in the United States.

▲ Walter P. Chrysler dies.

■ Chrysler introduces safety rim wheels on its 1940 models.

■ Germany bombs London, beginning what came to be called the "Blitz."

■ Duke Ellington reaches his height of fame as a jazz composer and pianist after returning from his band's tour of Europe.

■ Howard Florey develops penicillin as a practical antibiotic.

■ On Stalin's orders, the exiled Leon Trotsky is assassinated in Mexico.

American Dreams

"Concept cars," a term sometimes used interchangeably with "dream cars," "idea cars," "show cars" or "experimentals," are seldom intended for manufacture, but instead to give free play to the imaginations of designers, test the market for future designs or draw crowds to a company's current auto show. One of the first concept cars was created in 1939 by the flamboyant Harley Earl, the director of Art and Color at General Motors since 1927. After his Buick Y-Job was unveiled to the public at an auto show in 1940, other American auto-mobile companies were quick to pick up the challenge. Chrysler was among the first to respond.

In 1941, Chrysler built two concept cars: the Thunderbolt and the Newport. No mere flights of fancy, these automobiles were based on solid engineering and proven technology, as would be many of the advanced Chrysler design concepts in the coming years. Chrysler concept cars were usually automobiles that could have been built and in some cases, except for quirks of history and economics, would have been built. Instead, their radical designs and advanced features influenced future, less fanciful and more practi-

Still surprisingly fresh looking today, the 1941 Thunderbolt offered inside a leather-covered dash, door panels and seats plus backlit Lucite edging along the instrument dials, which made them glow at night. Under the hood was Chrysler's conventional inline eight-cylinder 323.5 cu. in. engine teamed with the Company's Fluid Drive transmission. Added to its streamlined looks, which Chrysler touted as "a new high in functional design," were its hidden headlamps, enclosed wheels and minimal trim made mostly of anodized aluminum.

cal production models—and not only at Chrysler.

Chrysler built six Thunderbolts based on an original design by Alex Tremulis and executed by Ralph Roberts, who worked with both Chrysler and the coach builder LeBaron. Inspired by the streamlined race cars of the day, the all-steel body of the Thunderbolt that rolled into auto shows was based on a Chrysler New Yorker chassis. It was lauded for its aerodynamic design and hailed as "The Car of the Future." Chrysler called the car a "convertible road-ster" because of its fully retractable, electrically controlled steel hardtop, which anticipated the Ford Skyliner by 16 years and the Mercedes SLK by half a century.

Like the Thunderbolts, only six Newports were built, and each was painted and trimmed differently. They shared the same engine and transmission. Like the Thunderbolts, the Newports came with push-button door handles and leather interior, and some were equipped with hidden headlamps. But there the similarities ended. The Newport was the natural evolution of the dual cowl phaeton popularized by independent coach builders in the 1930s. But the phaeton style was already passé, and while the Thunderbolt, even today, has about it the whiff of the modern, the Newport is redolent of the parades of days gone by.

▲ Willys-Overland begins production of the Model MB
Willys Jeep, delivering more
than 350,000 vehicles by the
end of World War II.

■ The U.S. government
establishes the Office of
Price Administration,
freezing the price of steel
and rationing rubber.

■ Orson Welles releases
Citizen Kane, according
to many the best movie
ever made.

▲ Joe DiMaggio hits in 56
consecutive games, estab-
lishing a major league
baseball record.

■ The top-secret Manhattan
Project begins work on an
atomic bomb.

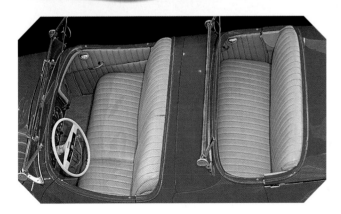

Basically a parade car, the 1940–1941 Newport, with its four doors, had no side windows, while both the front and rear windshields folded flat forward. Built on the long wheelbase of the Imperial chassis, the Newport had twin cockpits featuring full three-across seating. The six Newports, after they had served their promotional purposes, were sold to individuals. Actress Lana Turner bought one. The Newport used as a pace car for the Indianapolis 500 sits in the Indianapolis Hall of Fame Museum. The automobile shown here features sealed-beam headlamps with converted wire stone guards rather than the original hidden lights, a change made by a previous owner.

The Newport was selected as the pace car for the 1941 Indianapolis 500, the only time a nonproduction vehicle has held that honor.

▲ The Japanese attack Pearl Harbor, precipitating America's entry into World War II.

■ U.S. Saving Bonds go on sale for the first time.

▼ Chrysler halts car production in favor of war materiel during World War II. Among other things, Chrysler produces 397,209 trucks, 25,507 tanks, 3 billion cartridges and 175,000 engines, including the one below, before war's end.

■ Popular actress Carol Lombard dies in a plane crash en route to a war-bond drive.

■ The tide of the war in the Pacific changes when the U.S. Navy wins a conclusive victory at the Battle of Midway.

A World at War

The attack on Pearl Harbor not only led the United States to enter World War II, it also forged an America more unified than it had ever been before or, perhaps, would ever be again. Congress immediately gave President Franklin D. Roosevelt the declaration of war he requested along with unprecedented powers to mobilize the country's citizenry and industry. Even before America's entry into the war, Roosevelt had issued a plea to the country's industrial leaders to build an "arsenal of democracy" and had been pushing

Congress and the American public toward support of Great Britain then under siege by the Nazis. Fighting, in effect, an undeclared war in the Atlantic, the United States had intensified recruitment in the armed forces and boosted weapon, battleship, truck and airplane production, but its entry into the war raised such efforts to almost unimaginable new levels. The automobile industry played an important role in the transformation of America's production capacity into a massive war machine. In 1940, Roosevelt tapped former General Motors President William S. Knudsen to head the Office of Production Management, and

At the Detroit Tank Arsenal, the huge complex Chrysler constructed to handle wartime production, Chrysler built some 18,000 Sherman tanks. This M4A4 Sherman was more than 19.5 ft. long, had a battle weight of just under 70,000 lb., and could achieve a top speed of 25 mph.

"[I]t is the purpose of the nation to build now with all possible speed every machine, every arsenal, every factory that we need to manufacture for defense material....We have the men, the skill, the wealth, and above all, the will....We must be the great arsenal of democracy."

—FRANKLIN DELANO ROOSEVELT

Knudsen now in turn called on his fellow auto executives, old rivals, to join the fight. He phoned Chrysler President K. T. Keller on a Sunday morning and asked, "K. T., do you want to build tanks?"

Chrysler had already delivered 25,000 trucks to the Army in 1939, even with its assembly plant in Belgium hostage to the German blitz, and it delivered 413,000 more in various shapes and sizes before the war was over. But the morning after Knudsen's call, Keller and his aides showed up at the Army's Rock Island arsenal to inspect American tanks. Toting out 168 pounds of blueprints, the group returned to Detroit and began converting a Warren, Michigan, field into the Detroit Tank Arsenal. Production of the first tank began seven months later, and soon the factory was rolling out five 25-ton tanks in each eight-hour shift. By the end of 1941, Chrysler had built 729 General Grant M3 tanks. The Sherman 32-ton tank followed and later the 43-ton Pershing. The auto companies stopped making private vehicles in early 1942 and retooled for the war effort, and tanks became Chrysler Corporation's best-known wartime product. During the war years, the Company made 25,000 tanks all told.

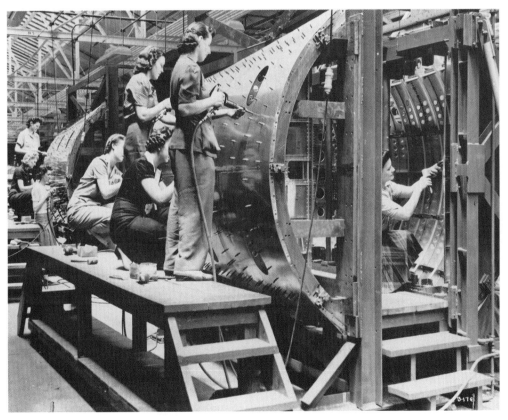

Chrysler women work here on one of the Martin B-26 fuselages (center section) the Company produced during the war.

In World War II, 16 million Americans, most of them men and ordinary citizens instead of professional soldiers, found themselves torn from their homes, their jobs and their families and thrust into a huge machine fighting a conflict in the far-flung reaches of the globe. Filling their places on the assembly line, women for the first time entered the work force in large numbers, a strange adventure of their own captured in this Chrysler wartime advertisement.

1942

■ Irving Berlin composes "White Christmas."

■ Leading a team of American scientists, Enrico Fermi triggers a self-sustaining atomic reaction, creating the world's first nuclear reaction.

1943

▲ Italy surrenders unconditionally to the invading Allies.

■ Jean-Paul Sartre publishes *Being and Nothingness,* a seminal statement of existentialism.

▼ The Allies begin strategic daytime (as well as nighttime) bombing of Nazi-occupied Europe.

▲ Allied forces invade Nazi-held Europe on "D-Day" in a final drive to defeat Germany.

■ The U.S. Congress passes the G. I. Bill.

■ DNA, the most basic genetic material, is discovered.

1945

▲ Allied troops liberate the prisoners of the Nazi concentration camps.

■ Representatives of 50 nations meet to draft a charter for the United Nations.

During World War II, a dozen Chrysler Corporation factories turned out a vast array of defense products in addition to the tanks for which it was noted—tugboats, aircraft engines and fuselages. And, once again, the Company produced a vast array of trucks.

Called "the fighting trucks," Dodge trucks such as these came off the assembly line ready to carry troops and equipment. Still others served as ambulances, small weapons carriers and reconnaissance vehicles.

At a new plant near Chicago, Dodge made Curtiss-Wright-developed R3350 engines (right) for the B-29 Superfortress like the one below. The Company also made nose sections (including controls) for the B-29s.

These "Victory" air raid sirens, with their gasoline engines, were independent of outside power supplies.

The Chrysler Marine Engine Division worked with Gar Wood Boat Company on Navy personnel boats. Chrysler also produced nearly 30,000 marine engines for military use. Sea Mule marine tugs and tractors, such as this one, may not have been glamorous, but they were much needed.

This drawing captures the range of Chrysler's wartime production.

During the war, Chrysler manufactured 60,000 40mm antiaircraft guns like this one, under license from Bofors, the Swedish armament company. Mounted singly on trailers, they were called "Bofors." Used aboard ships in pairs, they were dubbed "Pom-Poms" because of their alternating firing pattern.

In addition to B-29 engines, Dodge built other aircraft products: Curtiss Helldiver wing sections, parts of the Marauder fuselage and Corsair landing gear. Produced at this plant were nose and center sections for the Martin B-26 Bomber.

Modified Dodge trucks, such as this 1941 military Command Car, served any number of purposes.

Coming off the line are a few of the shells Chrysler produced during the war—some 3.25 billion rounds of small arms ammunition, 1.99 million 20mm shells, 328,000 explosive rockets and 101,000 incendiary bombs.

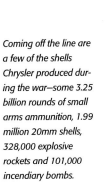

▲ "V-E Day" on May 8 marks the German surrender and ends the war in Europe.

■ At mid-year, Chrysler begins reconversion to car production; its first postwar cars come off the line in December.

▲ The U.S. Army Air Force drops atomic bombs on Japan resulting in a quick end to World War II.

■ Dodge introduces the Power Wagon, a civilian version of its four-wheel-drive army truck.

■ "Bebop" music becomes popular.

1946

■ Willys produces its civilian Jeep station wagon.

▲ Chrysler introduces its Town & Country convertible and sedan, replacing the wagon.

■ Scientists from the University of Pennsylvania direct the construction of the world's first entirely electronic computer.

■ Daimler-Benz produces its first postwar model, the four-cylinder 170V.

■ Charles Carlson invents Xerography process.

■ The U.S. Navy tests atomic bombs on Bikini Island.

▲ Kaiser Motors sells its first Kaisers and Frazers.

■ R. E. Byrd begins his expedition to the South Pole.

Peaceful Transition

By 1939, the U.S. military was gearing up for a war it knew was coming. The U.S. government had told automakers that it was looking for "a light reconnaissance vehicle" to replace the Army's motorcycle, and new Willys-Overland President Joseph W. Frazer began discussion of a "mosquito" car with government officials and provided sketches for the vehicle in December. Willys got the contract in 1941, calling its car the MA, and later the MB. But the Army, and the world, came to know it as the Jeep. Some claimed that the name came from the slurring of the letters *GP*, which were the military abbreviation for "General Purpose." Others say the car was named for a popular character called "Eugene the Jeep" in the *Popeye* cartoon strip. Whatever its origin, the name entered into the American lexicon and, for a while, served almost as a generic title for off-road vehicles, while the Jeep itself became an icon of the war. Its ubiquity at the front—Willys-Overland would build more than 368,000 vehicles, and Ford, under license, some 200,000, for the U.S. Army—saved the company and allowed it to return to passenger car production in a healthier state.

The "light reconnaissance vehicles" Willys-Overland produced for the U.S. Army during World War II, like this 1943 Jeep MB, remained emblematic of combat vehicles, recently joined in pop-culture iconography by the Hum-Vee.

Willys trademarked the name after the war and planned to turn the vehicle into an off-road utility vehicle for the farm. The Jeep served as the starting point for Willys-Overland's creation of the first all-steel station wagon, and station wagons in general became icons of the postwar suburban lifestyle just as the Jeep had been of Army life. Willys also used the Army Jeep as the basis for its inexpensive but "sporty" Jeepster, a forerunner of today's sport-utility vehicles.

In mid-war, Joseph Frazer left Willys and acquired control of Graham Motors. In 1945, Frazer joined shipbuilding tycoon Henry J. Kaiser to launch a new car company. Kaiser Manufacturing, a subsidiary of Kaiser-Frazer, purchased Willys-Overland in 1953 and renamed it Willys Motors. Although Kaiser-Frazer soon foundered, Kaiser expanded the market for the Jeep, and by the 1960s, the vehicle was manufactured in roughly 30 countries and was sold in 150. By then, Willys was known as Kaiser Jeep. In 1970, it was purchased by American Motors, and the Jeep, with some models hardly distinguishable in looks from the "light reconnaissance vehicle" the Army had purchased in the war, became a staple of that company, just as it would for Chrysler after it purchased American Motors in 1987.

As American Motors would later do with its Wagoneers and Cherokees, Willys used the Jeep as a basis for other models, such as the 1950 Jeepster shown above.

After the war, Willys turned the Jeep into an inexpensive off-road workhorse. The Jeep retained its basic design but was continually improved. Its steady sales led to the acquisition of Jeep by AMC. Above is the 1945 Willys CJ 2-A; at right a 1973 American Motors Jeep.

- The U.S. Congress passes the National Security Act, creating the Central Intelligence Agency (CIA).

- Jackie Robinson becomes the first African American to sign a contract with a major league baseball team.

- Hudson introduces the step-down design.

- Bell Laboratory scientists invent the transistor.

- Henry Ford dies.

- The "New Look" dominates fashion; its yards and yards of fabric signal a new era of prosperity and excess.

Peace and Prosperity

In February 1942, the United States government halted American automobile production and turned the industry to the war effort; the ban was not lifted until late 1945. Afterward, Chrysler—along with the rest of the industry—found it difficult to switch back from war goods to automobiles. A severe shortage of material meant that few cars were produced in the final months of 1945, and those that did roll off the assembly lines of American automakers were warmed-over 1942 models with cosmetic changes. Through 1948, Chrysler Corporation, too, sold such reheated leftovers, but it hardly mattered. GIs returning to the States with combat pay to spend and those on the home front who had had nothing new to buy throughout the war hardly noticed as they snapped up anything the automobile industry offered. The frenzy of postwar consumption kicked off a long wave of economic growth, which fed the amazing seller's market and offered automakers a potential unlike anything they had seen since the 1920s. It was in this atmosphere that Chrysler brought to showrooms perhaps the most distinctive car of the immediate postwar era: the Town & Country.

Chrysler was the last of the three major automakers to introduce new designs in the years following World War II. In 1949, it aimed at the new suburban market with the debut of the first all-steel Plymouth station wagon.

After World War II, Willys-Overland produced an all-metal-body station wagon, based on the Jeep, which it had developed and produced for the United States armed forces during the war. Station wagons had been, primarily, commercial vehicles. Willys pitched its new wagon as an accoutrement of suburban life. Like this 1949 model (above), the Jeep station wagon tried to capture the feel of the prewar wagons of the affluent by creating the illusion of a wood body. The stamped panels, however, did more than suggest the car's wooden-bodied predecessors; they also added strength and relieved the wagon's boxy shape.

Introduced as an estate wagon before World War II, the Town & Country returned after the war in sedan and convertible body styles that borrowed their basic wood bodies from the summer-home station wagons of the affluent. The sedan was the more distinctive of Chrysler's Town & Country models, with its extended luggage locker trunk, chrome-and-wood roof rack, interior wood-door trim panels, leather check straps and wood door framing and roof bows, but the Town & Country convertible was the height of postwar glamour.

Although the Town & County captured the aspirations of the prosperous American suburbanites,

Chrysler did not offer a Town & Country station wagon. The station wagon would have its day as the middle class moved to the suburbs. In 1946, Willys-Overland introduced the all-metal wagon based on its wartime Jeep, though its metal side panels imitated the wood veneers of older wagons. When Chrysler offered its first new models designed postwar, one of them, not coincidentally, was an all-steel station wagon, the 1949 Plymouth Suburban. The Town & Country, expensive to maintain and beyond the reach of most middle-class consumers, lasted a few more years, but the all-metal station wagon soon became the icon of suburban life.

1948

■ The U.S. Congress passes the Selective Service Act, requiring universal service in the military.

▼ The Berlin Airlift begins.

1949

■ Chrysler becomes the last of the Big Three to introduce new car designs in the postwar years.

■ Designer Virgil Exner joins Chrysler.

■ Nash makes a splash with its new Airflyte model.

■ Mao Tse-tung's Communists take control of mainland China and declare it the People's Republic of China.

■ The Soviet Union tests its first atomic bomb.

■ South Africa establishes apartheid—the "absolute separation between black and white citizens"—as national policy.

The postwar favorite of movie stars and celebrities, the Town & Country was mimicked by Ford, Mercury and even Nash, but none captured its panache. Chrysler built 8,368 convertibles through 1948, most—like the 1948 model shown here—with six-cylinder engines, along with 4,049 six-cylinder and 100 eight-cylinder sedans. The gleaming, tongue-in-groove woodwork had to be revarnished often, especially if left outdoors, and repairs were intricate and costly.

The Boom Time

Postwar Americans witnessed the largest real estate boom in history, a boom fueled by their need not only to return to normality after years of depression and war, but also to create the good life so many of them had dreamed about during the war. The new society rising out of the war-spawned prosperity needed the skills and training of the masses of new veterans. The newly passed G.I. Bill offered them the kind of education they could never have hoped for before the war. As they poured back onto American soil, many of these veterans did not return to the farms and small towns they had left four years earlier. Instead, they joined their wives and their friends who had moved into the cities to work for the high-paying war plants. They filled America's college classrooms, its new tract homes and its burgeoning airline, aerospace, automobile, communications, plastics, steel and service industries. The years of separation and hardship had given birth to new hope just as the veterans and their wealthy neighbors gave birth to a new generation, the largest in history, in what sociologists would soon be calling the baby boom.

Even the kind of houses they bought were a product of the war. The construction company of Levitt and Sons first experimented with the mass production of homes during World War II. Under government contract to build housing for war workers, the company had innovated prefabricated materials and assembly-line construction that cut costs and saved time. After the war, Levitt and Sons translated these advances to private home building, and by 1951, the company had used its precise 27-step process to construct Levittown in Hempstead, New York, where it created more than 30 homes a day. Middle-class families poured into these and other such suburban tract homes with the help of easy credit terms made possible by funds from the Federal Housing Administration and the Veterans Administration.

Since these houses lay outside urban areas where most of the high-paying jobs were located, individual transportation became a necessity, and the new suburbanites bought extra cars to drive to and fro on the new limited-access highways springing up for that purpose. By the middle of the decade, the government was helping to build those highways and connect them to one another in a major new interstate system. Suburbanites now used the roads not just to go to work and back but to visit the folks or to take the family out for a meal or on a vacation. New chains of businesses popped up to service this traffic—Holiday Inns and Howard Johnsons replaced the old "tourist camps" of earlier decades; fast food franchises like McDonalds mushroomed across the country; shopping malls replaced downtowns; and even vacation spots took on a new odor with the opening of Disneyland in suburban California.

At first the postwar sellers' market in automobiles had swelled the bottom lines of not just the Big Three but also the Little Five—as the independents were known—and even encouraged newcomers to get into the business. But as the suburbanites filled their homes with ever more modern, usually electronic conveniences, from can openers to refrigerators to televisions, consumption became conspicuous, and the sellers' market turned into the kind of heated competition last seen

in the 1920s. Only now the UAW, having gained power in the industry during the war, also insisted its members share in the wealth. After some early postwar strikes, the automakers generally came to terms with the unions, offering retirement packages and standard-of-living increases. But the change would cost the consumer. Instead of increased competition creating better cars, as it had in the 1920s, it now produced a cheap excess. Detroit flourished by producing brand name cars covered in chrome, sprouting fins, loaded with extras and sporting ever more powerful V-8 engines—cars, in short, in which owners were proud to be seen by the neighbors and ones they would soon be sure to trade in on even gaudier new models. The horsepower and the gadgets and the conformity were rough on the independents. Packard merged with Studebaker and was gone by decade's end. Hudson joined Nash to create American Motors, and both names were replaced by the compact Rambler. The revolutionary Tucker built a mere 50 cars,

and the brash Henry Kaiser found he could only profit building Jeep vehicles.

Having made it, the Americans huddling around the tube to catch *Ozzie and Harriet* and *Leave It to Beaver* became both cautious and status conscious. They elected Dwight Eisenhower to the presidency and Joe McCarthy to the Senate. They feared falling behind the Joneses at home and the Russians abroad. They worried that eggheads and Communists were out to take away their good life and that Elvis Presley and the beatniks wanted to corrupt their children. In response, their children, naturally enough, became rebels without a cause, duck-tailed juveniles and hot-rodders driving souped-up versions of whatever old cars they could afford to buy. For even restless youth could not escape the car culture that had taken hold of America in the 1950s. Elvis Presley celebrated his new-found fame and fortune by buying pink Cadillacs; James Dean his by dying in a Porsche. Alienated teenagers everywhere cruised the strip listening to rock-and-roll on the radio and clogged the local drive-in hamburger joints after school and drive-in movies on Saturday night.

It was hardly surprising that in an era when a car's appearance rather than its engineering features became the primary selling point, the stylist should hold the upper hand in Detroit. To GM's chief stylist Harley Earl, who had been smitten by the Lockheed P-38 fighter plane with its twin tail wings, usually goes the credit for the first ground-borne versions of those fins. From the modest bumps of the 1948 Cadillac, Earl's fins had soared ever more prominently and swept downward through the other GM divisions. The 1959 Cadillac might well be the very essence of American Cold War swagger, but long before then Virgil Exner, the creator of the novel 1947 Studebaker, had moved to Chrysler and initiated the "Forward Look" with "Flite-Sweep" styling, replete with multitoned flashiness and fins and flairs of every description. The epitome of 1950's design excess, however, belongs by general consensus to the decade's greatest flop—the 1958 Ford Edsel.

The Edsel was a turning point.

For sure, there had always been that uneasiness just beneath the snug surface of suburban life. The Korean War, which had not quite been a war but a "police action," ended in a cease fire, which was not quite a win but a withdrawal. After the Russians had tested their first atomic bomb in 1949, the U.S. had responded by building a hydrogen bomb in 1952, only to have the Russians respond with their own H-bomb in 1955. As parents sank fall-out shelters in the backyards of their dream homes, the kids at school practiced duck-and-cover during air raid drills after watching graphic films about the kind of destruction such bombs caused.

Then, too, there had always been those who failed to share in the postwar boom. As early as 1954, the Supreme Court had tried to redress some of the burden under which African Americans had been suffering by outlawing segregation in public education. In 1955, an African American woman named Rosa Parks had refused to give up her seat and move to the back of a Montgomery, Alabama, bus. Her arrest had kicked off a boycott that signaled a renewed struggle for civil rights by African Americans. In 1957, federal troops were called out to enforce the integration of schools in Little Rock, Arkansas, when brick-throwing white crowds tried to prevent it.

But two months before the Edsel's appearance, the nation plummeted into a sharp economic recession that affected all car sales. A month after it first rolled off the line, the Soviets put their first *Sputnik* in orbit, shocking Americans and shaking their faith it the country's once highly touted technology. That same year small imports, mainly Volkswagen Beetles, for the first time in 50 years made a significant dent in the American market. Added to the sales of the compact Rambler (which, by 1960 would be the third best-selling car in America), small cars had seized 12 percent of the market. A year later, the Cuban Revolution established a Communist government 10 miles off the shores of the United States. By the end of 1959, New York Governor Nelson Rockefeller was proposing to fund a system of public shelters to protect U.S. citizens from radioactive fallout following a nuclear attack. As Europe rebounded from the last world war and stepped up its exports, as social unrest in the United States gained momentum, as the Cold War malaise ate away at the good life, American uneasiness grew manifest. The excesses of a car like the Edsel—perfect perhaps for 1955 when it was conceived—seemed by 1958 more bluster than an affirmation of the vaunted status quo's peace and prosperity.

■ Diners Club introduces the credit card.

■ The U.S. Senate, led by Tennessee's Estes Kefauver, opens hearings to investigate organized crime.

▲ U.S. Senator Joseph P. McCarthy begins a four-year "witch-hunt" for Communists in government and industry.

■ The number of televisions in American homes increases to 15 million from 1.5 million sets the year before.

■ William Faulkner, the most prominent author of the Southern Literary Renaissance, wins the Nobel Prize for literature.

▼ The United States joins United Nations forces in a police action to repel Communist North Korean advances into South Korea.

Changing of the Guard

In the autumn of 1950, Kaufman Thuma "K. T." Keller turned over the presidency of Chrysler Corporation to Lester Lum "Tex" Colbert. The year before, Chrysler's long awaited postwar models had finally appeared, but anyone expecting a radical about-face in styling was sorely disappointed. Keller had ascended to the presidency of the Company in 1935, after having been groomed for the position for years. Becoming president in the midst of the Airflow debacle, he was ever after leery of abrupt styling change. While Ford and GM were rolling out slick and rakish new shapes, Chrysler—under admonition from Keller to design cars for men wearing hats—stuck to the high profile form of prewar days. Keller might accept the reshaping of a grille here or the reworking of some chrome there, but what he really wanted, he said, was to produce good cars that made good money.

And, indeed, his cars, for all their lack of panache, did make money: *Fortune* magazine noted in 1948 that Chrysler was "never so rich." As the 1940s drew to a close, new investments fueled a major plant expansion. New factories soon to come on line in New Orleans, Louisiana; Newark, Delaware; and Trenton, Michigan,

Taking office just after the dramatic introduction of the Airflow—of which he was a critic—shook the Company's confidence, K. T. Keller was a conservative executive. In early 1942, domestic automakers ceased producing cars because of the war. Production resumed postwar with the warmed-over prewar models. By 1949 all the automakers had introduced new models. Chrysler's, the last introduced, drew on work done during the war, and by their introduction in 1949 already seemed dated. Below is a 1941 Chrysler Imperial; at lower right, one of the Company's "new models," a 1949 New Yorker.

When K. T. Keller became Chrysler Corporation chairman after 15 years as Company president, he had come a long way from his modest roots in rural Pennsylvania. Born near Lancaster in 1885, he apprenticed as a mechanic at Westinghouse before heading to Detroit and work in the auto industry. He first met Walter P. Chrysler in 1912, when both men were employed by GM, and in 1917, Chrysler hired Keller as a master mechanic for Buick. As Chrysler retired from GM and later was hired to rescue Willys-Overland, he promised to call the young mechanic someday with a better job offer. Keller, who meanwhile had risen in the industry to vice president and general manager of GM-Canada, got the call in 1926. Keller left GM on the spot to become vice president in charge of manufacturing for the brand new Chrysler Corporation.

would manufacture Chrysler's soundly engineered products in ever increasing numbers. Comfortably in the number two spot among American auto companies, Chrysler saw 1949 sales rise in every division except DeSoto. Up 110,000 from 1948, they amounted in total to almost 1 million automobiles. And in 1950, even a three-month strike failed to keep sales from reaching 1.25 million cars. With Dodge trucks topping 125,000 that same year, Keller claimed that but for the strike his Company would have sold 1.5 million vehicles. Profits too were up, since Chrysler Corporation had the lowest unit costs and best profit margin in the industry.

By 1950, Keller could look back with pride on his accomplishments at Chrysler, secure in the knowledge that he was turning over not merely a profitable enterprise, but one with a bright future. In addition to the sales and the expansions, Chrysler had—ready for installation in its 1951 models—a new V-8 engine with hemispherical combustion chambers that promised to stand the industry on its ear. Accepting an offer to head up the U.S. missile program after the outbreak of the Korean War, Keller remained on Chrysler's board as chairman, but he let go the reins. The Company was Colbert's to make of it what he would.

A domestic version of World War II's workhorse was introduced to the postwar public as the Dodge Power Wagon. Three-quarter-ton trucks like the 1954 model shown here began rolling off the line in 1946. Produced for more than 20 years, the Power Wagon was the ultimate indomitable off-road vehicle.

L. L. "Tex" Colbert became president of Chrysler Corporation in 1950.

The 1940 Dodge 1/2-ton pickup at left was part of a new series introduced in 1939 and dubbed "job-rated." Chrysler's postwar truck models seemed more successful than the automobiles, since high profile was not a drawback in a truck. In 1949, Dodge introduced the first new trucks in a decade. Its 1/2-ton pickups, like the one at right, came with high-visibility "pilot house" cabs.

1950

▲ Workers at Chrysler's assembly plants stage a 104-day strike to protect their pensions.

■ Nash Motors introduces a compact Rambler.

■ K. T. Keller becomes chairman of Chrysler, the first to assume the title since Walter P. Chrysler's death in 1940.

■ Willys registers the Jeep trademark in the United States and internationally.

1951

■ Color television is introduced.

■ J. D. Salinger publishes *The Catcher in the Rye*, which becomes the bedrock text about alienated youth.

Fifties FirePower

Chrysler's reputation for excellent engineering was well established by the 1950s, but the Company outdid itself in 1951 with the introduction of a new engine that quickly acquired legendary status. The 331 cu. in. V-8 FirePower engine, first developed by Ray White, William E. Drinkard and Mel Carpentier under the guidance of James C. Zeder (brother of Fred Zeder and a well-respected engineer in his own right), was known as the "Hemi" (from the hemispherical shape of its combustion chambers).

Chrysler's 1951 owner's manual boasted the engine was "one of the most important 'firsts' in the automobile industry," although development of the engine actually dated back to 1935 when Chrysler engineers began seriously to look for more horsepower. The basic hemi-head design had been around for years on exotic racing cars. Chrysler, however, was the first to make it practical for production models. With a compression ratio of 7.5:1 and rated at 180 hp at 4,000 rpm, the Hemi was, from the start, the most powerful engine around—more powerful than any of the postwar overhead engines developed by the Big Three automakers and some 20 hp more powerful than Cadillac's V-8 of the same displacement.

In advertisements for the Chrysler New Yorker, the Company touted the new FirePower V-8 Hemi engine and the choice of the vehicle as the pace car for the 1951 Indianapolis 500.

Unlike the previously introduced General Motors' engines, which used wedge-shaped combustion chambers with valves placed side by side on the sloping roof and spark plugs placed at the peak of the wedge, Chrysler's Hemi in effect topped each cylinder with a scooped-out dome-shaped head. One intake valve and one exhaust valve lay on opposite sides of the dome with the spark plug located very near the center of the combustion chamber. The engine head was more complex and expensive to produce, but its advantages were better breathing, more complete combustion and a higher compression ratio without knock for a more effective fuel-air mix and for less heat loss. This permitted more horsepower. The cutaway view in the above advertisement shows the combustion chamber, the large and widely spaced valves and the centrally located spark plug.

But Chrysler actually showed up late in the horsepower race. Ford's flat-head V-8 debuted in 1932, but the overhead V-8 engine did not appear until the 1952 Lincoln. General Motors introduced its first overhead V-8 in 1949, although a flat-head V-8 appeared earlier. In the late 1940s, Chrysler engineers were still secretly concentrating on a new cylinder head design. Recognizing that higher compression ratios were their best route to more power, the engineers focused on the shape of the combustion chamber, the arrangement of overhead valves and the location of the spark plug. Their hemispherical head, which allowed for bigger valves to help the combustion chamber breathe, for a centrally located spark plug creating quicker, more even ignition and for reduced engine knock to help boost compression ratio, produced an engine that exceeded the power of GM's new overhead V-8.

An instantly popular off-the-shelf racing engine, the Hemi came to dominate the National Association for Stock Car Auto Racing (NASCAR) circuit and became the favorite of stock car and drag racers. As the most powerful engine available for passenger cars, the Hemi fueled the growth of Chrysler's "muscle car" models in the coming decades.

Introduced in 1951, the Twin-H engine, with its two single barrels and manifold, appears here in the Walter P. Chrysler Museum's 1953 Hudson Hornet club coupe. The engine dominated stock car racing until 1955, when the Chrysler 300 arrived on the scene.

Not until the era of the muscle cars would Hemis become widely available in lower-cost production models, but this 1957 Plymouth Fury hardtop coupe boasted a Poly-Sphere engine known as the "Poor Man's Hemi," the biggest V-8 in its field. Available only as a two-door in Sand Dune white finish with gold anodized aluminum "sport tone" trim insets, the Fury packaged style, luxury and power with high performance.

1952

▲ Daimler-Benz debuts the 300 SL (gull wing) coupe.

■ Nash Motors debuts its Healey sports cars and the Metropolitan.

■ Chrysler's Ted Cunningham begins competing at Le Mans and on the stock car circuit in cars equipped with Hemi engines.

1953

▲ World War II hero Dwight D. Eisenhower becomes president of the United States.

■ Ian Fleming publishes *Casino Royale*, the first James Bond adventure.

■ Julius and Ethel Rosenberg, convicted of turning over atomic secrets to the Soviet Union, are executed.

■ Chrysler offers its first
  cars with automatic
  transmissions.

■ A merger of Hudson and
  Nash becomes American
  Motors; AMC President
  George Mason dies, and
  George Romney takes over.

■ The fighting ends in Korea.

■ The CIA backs the Shah of
  Iran, signaling a new era of
  cloak-and-dagger meddling
  in the affairs of other
  countries.

■ In *Brown v. Topeka Board
  of Education*, the U.S.
  Supreme Court strikes
  down segregation, launching the 20th century's struggle for civil rights in earnest.

▼ *I Love Lucy* becomes television's top-rated show.

New in the Fifties

In 1951, Chrysler introduced power steering, adding to its impressive string of engineering firsts. Power steering allowed hydraulics to do 85 percent of the work in turning the wheels and removed the last intimidation that driving held for women. Instead of the series of mechanical linkages that transferred to the wheels the physical force drivers used when turning a traditionally steered car, power steering used a pump to supply pressure to a control valve. This valve directed the pressure to pistons that assisted the driver in steering the vehicle. The reduced effort made for "finger-tip" driving.

Chrysler was not always first in new features, of course, and sometimes it was among the last, but when the Company did engage the competition, it frequently demonstrated how the feature should have worked from the beginning. Take air-conditioning, for example. Chrysler was a leader in full-building air-conditioning in the New York Chrysler Building, but it was slow to adapt its experience to cars. Instead, Packard first attempted air-conditioned autos in 1940, and Cadillac a year later. By the time Chrysler came to the market with the feature in 1954, air-conditioning was widely available. But its Air-

Torsion-bar springs like those in the illustration at right were first fitted on all Chrysler car models in 1957. Torsion bars replaced conventional coil springs, allowing for better handling and the low-slung look of Virgil Exner's designs.

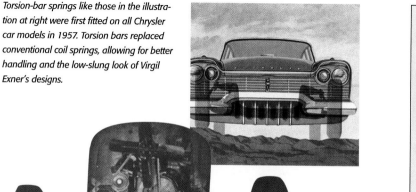

Oriflow shock absorbers automatically compensated for a full range of road conditions from sudden jolts to mild bumps.

In the early 1950s, Chrysler continued to tout its innovations and engineering excellence, as in these advertisements for its new Hydraguide Power Steering and PowerFlite.

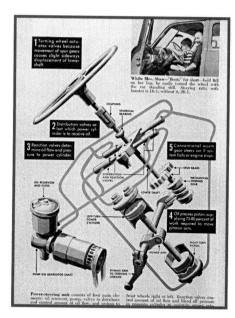

The diagram above shows the workings of Chrysler's innovative hydraulic power steering system.

Temp system was less complicated and more efficient than any other, its cool-down rate quicker and—since it used more outside air than the competition's—Chrysler's cabin air felt less "artificial" and stale. Similarly, Chrysler was late in offering a fully automatic transmission, but when it did in 1953, the PowerFlite transmission had fewer parts, providing smooth shifting and excellent acceleration. Three years later, Chrysler introduced a push-button controlled transmission.

On the other hand, Chrysler had always been a leader in automobile suspension, and a new shock absorber, the Oriflow, appeared in 1951. Its design is still reflected in today's shocks. Pushed on by design stylist Virgil Exner's need for low hood and roof lines, in 1957 Chrysler engineers introduced torsion-bar springs and "Total Contact Brakes," both of which brought drivers the benefits of remarkable handling. The next year saw the first cruise control, the "Auto-Pilot Speed-Warning & Control System." In warning mode, it increased accelerator back-pressure at a predetermined speed; in control mode, it operated just as today's systems do. Modern electronic cruise control is simpler and perhaps more accurate, but Chrysler again showed what could be done with automobile technology.

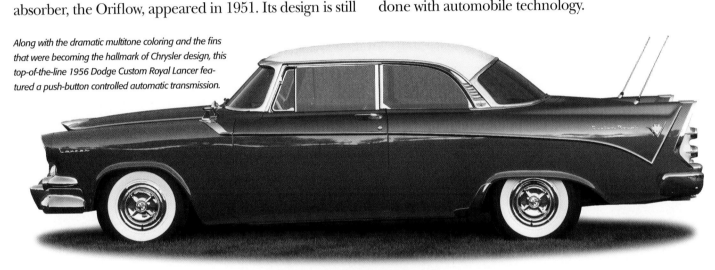

Along with the dramatic multitone coloring and the fins that were becoming the hallmark of Chrysler design, this top-of-the-line 1956 Dodge Custom Royal Lancer featured a push-button controlled automatic transmission.

The 1951 New Yorker, shown here in its convertible model, boasted the powerful new Hemi engine and was the first American production car with power steering and the improved shock absorbers dubbed "Oriflow."

1954

■ Kaiser acquires Willys-Overland, which becomes Willys Motors.

▲ Chrysler opens its 4,000-acre Engineering Proving Grounds at Chelsea, Michigan.

■ Kaiser-Willys introduces the CJ-5 Jeep; the model remains in production until 1983.

■ Joe McCarthy is censored by the U.S. Senate for turning his Communist witch hunt on the U.S. Army, bringing his influence to an end.

1955

■ Jonas Salk's vaccine for polio receives government approval.

▲ The arrest of Rosa Parks, an African American patron of the Montgomery, Alabama, city bus system, initiates a bus boycott, which ends when the buses are integrated.

■ Walt Disney opens Disneyland in Anaheim, California.

■ Ray Kroc founds the McDonald's Corporation, developing a chain of hamburger stands that eventually numbered more than 10,000 worldwide.

■ Kaiser and Willys marques are discontinued. Only Jeep remains as a product of Willys Motors of Kaiser Industries Corp.

▲ Chrysler debuts the "Forward Look" in its cars.

■ Chrysler introduces the Chrysler 300 and makes its Imperial model a separate line.

■ The AFL and the CIO merge, and George Meany becomes the new labor organization's president.

■ The first atomic power plant goes on line in Schenectady, New York.

At the Track

In 1950, millionaire sportsman Briggs Cunningham turned to his friend, Chrysler President K. T. Keller, and arranged to buy a prototype of the Company's FirePower V-8, the 331 cu. in. Hemi engine, for his team of sports cars. At Le Mans in 1951, Cunningham entered three C-2 roadsters designed around the Hemi, highly modified and dyno tested by Chrysler engineers. One of these cars ran second for six hours before throwing a rod. Cunningham was back in 1952 with a 300 hp C-4RK coupe and two C-4 roadsters (in addition to their Hemis, all three were equipped with new Chrysler rear axles).

One of the roadsters finished fourth. The next year was sensational, with Cunningham's cars taking third, seventh and tenth, followed in 1954 by a third and fifth place with a pair of 310 hp C-4Rs clocking 160 mph in a torrential downpour. But the costs, at the time, seemed astronomical, and thereafter Cunningham confined his C-4s, the darlings of American sports car racing, to American contests, winning at Watkins Glen, Sebring, Road America and a number of other major Sports Car Club of America (SCCA) events in the 1950s.

The decade, too, proved a good one for Chrysler stock car teams. Lee Petty had already claimed a good share of the National Association for Stock Car Auto

The Chrysler Hemi engine, having proved itself on the race track, powered the limited-edition, high-performance Chrysler 300 shown here.

Racing (NASCAR) purses in his home-built Plymouth when Johnny Mantz took the first Southern 500 at the Darlington raceway in 1950 with a six-cylinder Plymouth. In 1954, Petty drove a Hemi-powered Chrysler to seven wins and 17 top finishes on the way to the NASCAR championship. Chrysler's first NASCAR title, this win broke the lock Oldsmobile and Hudson had previously enjoyed on the championship. But it was Mercury Outboard Company impresario Carl Kiekhaefer's stock car team that dominated NASCAR in the mid-1950s. Fielded around the new Chrysler 300, Kiekhaefer's team of drivers won 20 out of 40 NASCAR events in 1955, and the 300s became the scourge of the class. Although Lee

Petty, driving a 300 and occasionally a Hemi-powered Dodge, gave them a run for the money, it was team driver Tim Flock who won the National Championship (equivalent to today's Winston Cup). When Flock, put off by Kiekhaefer's abrasiveness, quit the team in 1956, Buck Baker won the championship, and two other team drivers—Herb Thomas and Speedy Thompson—came in ahead of fourth-place Petty. By then other teams, disturbed by Kiekhaefer's success (50 wins in 92 starts in two years) were clamoring for rule changes. With little left to prove and with skyrocketing costs, Kiekhaefer dropped out of racing, disbanding what some have argued was the best team in stock car racing history.

Briggs Cunningham made his mark at Le Mans in the 1950s with a series of sports cars, like this 1953 C-5R, powered by Chrysler Hemi engines.

With the development of its new Hemi engine, Chrysler entered the horsepower race with a roar, which it made sure its customers heard through ads like these, touting Chrysler as the "finest engineered cars in the world."

■ Tensions in the Middle East explode over the Suez Canal.

■ Hungary revolts against Soviet influence in its internal affairs.

▲ The U.S. Congress passes the Interstate Highway Act of 1956.

■ American Motors drops its Rambler compact and offers the Nash Cross Country Wagon, the first "hardtop" station wagon.

■ Dodge's Daytona 500 Hemi model is introduced.

▼ Elvis Presley, a symbol of a cultural revolution among young people, appears on Sunday night television's *Ed Sullivan Show.*

■ The Italian liner *Andrea Doria* sinks after a collision, and with it goes the Chrysler Norseman show car just built in Italy.

▲ U.S. federal troops force public schools in Little Rock, Arkansas, to integrate.

■ Chrysler cars feature new styling with fins and a low profile created by replacing spring suspension with a torsion bar.

■ Chrysler attains the highest market share it will enjoy for the next 39 years.

1958

■ The U.S. establishes the National Aeronautics and Space Administration (NASA).

■ American Motors drops the Nash name from its full-sized line in favor of the Rambler; the old sub-compact called Rambler reappears as the Rambler American.

The Forward Look

Under Company President K. T. Keller, Chrysler in the postwar era continued to emphasize engineering over style in its design of new models. And in the early 1950s, engineering advances such as power steering and the legendary, lusty hemi-head FirePower V-8 engine still brought in customers at a time when the Company's styling group remained small and could do little more than decorate the boxy style upon which Keller insisted. Then Chrysler lost its number two position in the industry to a fast-rising Ford, and Keller, approaching retirement, decided to do something about Chrysler's styling malaise.

In 1949, Chrysler hired the talented Virgil Exner away from Studebaker to head an advanced styling section free of the Company's Engineering and Product Design operations. Named director of Styling in 1953, Exner took the design department from a staff of 17 to more than 280 by 1955, the first year his new design theme, which was soon called "the Forward Look," began to transform dowdy Plymouths and Dodges into sleek, sculptured and more colorful machines. Exner pushed the sleeker 1955 look and the modestly finned

Hired in 1949 to head advanced design, Virgil Exner (far left) became Chrysler's first vice president of Styling and took automobile design in new directions. Establishing Styling on a par roughly equal to Engineering at Chrysler, he changed the very process by which the Company's cars were designed. Today's Product Design Office grew, for the most part, from the organization Exner first put in place.

"**The corporation is now placing its huge bets on stylists' ideas of design, rather than the stern and sensible concepts of engineers.**"

—FORTUNE, 1954

Considered one of Virgil Exner's finest designs, the Flite Sweep styling of this 1957 Imperial Southampton featured the iconic tail fins and "gunsight" tail lamps. Its curved side window glass, now an industry standard, was a Chrysler first introduced on the 1957 Imperials. This was one of the 1957 Chrysler models that won awards from the Industrial Designers Institute.

and tail-lifted designs of 1956 into Chrysler's second attack—after the Airflow design of the 1930s—on the basic architecture of the American automobile.

It was in 1957, however, that the first real Exner cars, dubbed "Flite Sweep," really stunned both the industry and the buying public. Encouraged by Keller's successor, L. L. "Tex" Colbert, Exner was aided by Engineering's new torsion-bar suspension (which allowed for much lower heights after Exner pushed for lower hood and roof lines).

Dramatically low-slung, Exner's new models had thin, flat roofs in cross-section that were supported by slim pillars and boasted a large increase in glass surfaces. Imperials had curved-glass side windows, an industry first that has become standard. And then there were the famous fins. The Plymouth's new rudders, the flying wedges of the DeSoto, New Yorker and Imperial and the folded swan wings of the Dodge in time became symbols of the period and classic American designs. Following the shock of the new Exner cars, the entire industry moved swiftly to lower heights and bigger fins. Chrysler's radical 1957 models garnered the Industrial Designers Institute gold medal for the cars and Exner's promotion to vice president of Styling.

Virgil Exner's new models were more colorful than their predecessors. Chrysler offered a total of 56 solid colors, 173 two-tone patterns, such as the one on this rare 1957 Plymouth four-door hardtop, and even three-tone options.

Tail fins accentuated the wedge shape that was the symbol of the Exner era in automobile design. But there were fins and then there were fins. The dramatic sweep of the fins on this 1957 Chrysler 300 C sport coupe took away none of its chaste simplicity. America's most powerful production car, the longer, lower two-door carried under its hood a Hemi engine enlarged to 392 cu. in. and enjoyed a cruising speed of 100 mph. Thanks to torsion-bar front suspension, some of Chrysler's two-door cars were as much as 5 in. lower than previous models.

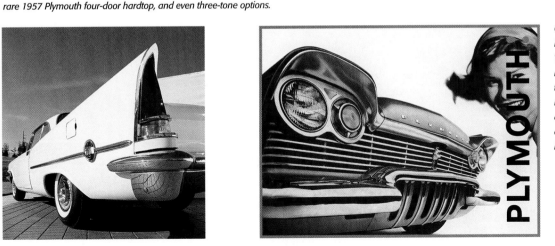

Called "the Forward Look," Virgil Exner's new design theme dominated Chrysler's automobile advertisements in the late 1950s.

1958

▲ The "Beatnik" movement begins in California and spreads throughout the United States.

■ Chrysler purchases a share in SIMCA Motors.

1959

▲ A revolution in Cuba, led by Fidel Castro, establishes a Communist regime a mere 90 miles from American soil.

■ Americans go underground when government officials propose the construction of family fallout shelters to protect against nuclear attack.

■ Hawaii becomes the 50th state in the nation.

■ Chrysler imports SIMCAs for sale in the United States.

The Turbulent Ride

In 1961, when President John F. Kennedy, the youngest man to hold the office and the first born in the 20th century, called on Americans in his inaugural address to ask what they could do for their country, he struck a cord with the young people of the nation. In a generation marked by idealism, twentysomethings joined the Peace Corps and headed off to points around the globe to spread the gospel of American democracy. By the time Kennedy was assassinated three years later, he had managed to heighten Cold War tensions with the botched Bay of Pigs invasion, his nuclear brinksmanship over Soviet-deployed missiles in Cuba and involvement in what became an undeclared war in Southeast Asia. Even as the Berlin Wall was being constructed, many of the idealistic youngsters Kennedy inspired had traveled not to foreign lands but to the American South, where they engaged in the growing struggle of black citizens for basic civil rights. Some used the lessons learned there to launch the Berkeley Free Speech movement, which in turn served as the training ground for the "New Mobilization" against the Vietnam War that the best and the brightest of Kennedy's aides continued to execute.

From the Poor People's March on Washington the summer before Kennedy's assassination to the Woodstock rock concert the summer after Lyndon Johnson had abandoned the presidency in 1968, the 1960s was a decade of mass gatherings and public confrontation, of Freedom Rides and lunch-counter sit-ins, of marches on Selma and the Pentagon, of black riots in Watts and police riots in Chicago. From the murders of three civil rights workers in Mississippi to the Hells Angels' knifing of a black youth at the Rolling Stones's Altamont concert, it was a decade of social and political violence—Medgar Evers gunned down in Jackson, four young black girls blown up in a church in Birmingham, JFK killed in Dallas, Malcolm X murdered in Harlem, Martin Luther King shot dead in Memphis, Robert Kennedy assassinated in Los Angeles. The forces of order—local police, the FBI, the CIA, the National Guard—grew more repressive as the forces of protest—the Southern Leadership Conference, CORE, SNCC, the Yippies, SDS, the Black Panthers—moved from passive resistance to change by any means necessary. First draft cards then city neighborhoods went up in flames as the civil turbulence pitted not so much brother against brother as mother and father against son and daughter. A generational struggle turned the baby boomers into the Counter Culture and the postwar establishment into the Silent Majority.

Not only the idealism and anger of the civil rights movement and the antiwar protests fueled the youth culture. There was also a sexual revolution underway, courtesy of the newly introduced birth control pill, which led young people to practice what they called "free love" and what their shocked parents considered immoral licentiousness. Just as disturbing to those parents were the drugs. The kids, it seemed, were experimenting with all kinds of altered states. Hippies who had learned to mellow out on marijuana from the Beat Generation of the late 1950s now added a whole

GIRLS SAY YES

to boys who say NO

Proceeds from the sale of this poster go to The Draft Resistance.

new category with psychedelics such as LSD, first developed by the CIA. The problem was not so much that everybody was taking such drugs—most probably did not, and those who did only did so occasionally—but that the new youth culture promoted drug use, if only as yet another dart lobbed at the Establishment in the name of freedom. Finally, there was the music. From the beginning with Elvis Presley, rock-and-roll had been associated with alienation and rebellion, and in the early 1960s, a new folk music, associated with Bob Dylan, consciously aired the growing protest against social injustice. By the time the Beatles landed on American shores and created a craze for English rock groups, popular music was expressly aimed at disaffected youth. Rock often explored sexual themes and ultimately glorified drug use—in a coded language, for sure, but clear enough to shock, once again, many older listeners. The Beatles, who started out wanting to hold your hand,

later tried to turn you on and tune you in. They then dropped out altogether to become cheeky subversives.

But, as the media pundits of the 1960s never hesitated to point out, the Counter Culture was a product not of the poor and disenfranchised but of the wealthier children of the middle class. They had money from home to spend, and they drove the Mustangs and Volkswagen buses they had taken to college to park in the mud and the mayhem outside Max Yagur's farm near Woodstock. As frequently as they listened to the Rolling Stones or the Animals, they also tuned in Jan and Dean and the Beach Boys—California surfing groups whose music sang of the glories of beach parties, surfer chicks and muscle cars. In fact, the Mustang—the brainchild, after all, of a middle-aged Ford executive named Lee Iacocca—became the car of the decade only because of the wealth of the baby boomers, who formed the perfect market for Detroit's new "pony cars."

For the suburban families from which most of the socially engaged rebels hailed were now buying second, third, even fourth cars: a sporty number for Dad, a station wagon for Mom, a compact for Sis to drive to school, a muscle car for Junior to impress the girls. The proliferation of models in the 1960s—Chevy alone offered 46 models, 32 engines, 20 transmissions, 21 colors (plus nine more in two tones) and upwards of 400 accessories and options—added an entirely new dimension to Alfred Sloan's vow to provide a car for every purse and purpose. Such diversity also proved to be Detroit's answer to market saturation. If sales still fluctuated from year to year, the general trend (in contrast to the 1950s) was upward, hitting a high of nearly 10 million in 1965. Among them were Detroit's reaction to a growing taste for

Smog-filled scenes such as the one shown at left led to the 1965 Vehicle Air Pollution and Control Act.

smaller cars—the Ford Falcon, the Chevy Corvair and Chrysler's Valiant. With so many cars and kinds of cars on the road, it was inevitable that one of them would sooner or later collide with the social conscience of the decade.

Like many of the protests of the 1960s, criticism of the auto industry and the car culture had been building throughout the 1950s. Here and there attacks had been made on what critics considered the chrome confections coming out of Detroit, the hucksters who sold them and the eye and air pollution they produced. A number of civic-minded critics broadened the attack to include what they viewed as the excessive boosterism of highway planners, and they especially complained about the mushrooming casualties in automobile accidents. But the movement took real shape around a Connecticut lawyer named Ralph Nader and his 1965 book, *Unsafe at Any Speed: The Designed-in Dangers of the American Automobile,* whose prime target was GM's Corvair. Little matter that the car was an easy target—even *Car and Driver* called it "one of the nastiest-handling cars ever built"—or that Detroit was hardly guilty of every charge in Nader's blanket indictment. It did not help that GM was so willing to play the villain and sic detectives on a man who apparently had no vices. By the time GM President John Roche was summoned before a Senate committee and forced to defend his product and to apologize publicly to Nader, the damage was done. An industry that had long avoided the kind of minute government regulation visited on other modes of transportation like railroads and airplanes was now on its way to being one of the most regulated in America.

That one of the more lasting legacies of the social protests of the 1960s should be a consumers' rights movement focused squarely on the automobile was a fitting if surprising end to the decade. Both the youthful rebels from the middle class and the American auto industry had spent the decade riding a long wave of prosperity. That wave was about to break. What loomed ahead—to use the language of the 1960s surf music—was a wipeout.

1960

- Chrysler enters the compact car market with the Valiant.

- Orally administered contraceptives are made available for the first time in the United States; before the year is out, 1 million women are using the birth control pill.

▲ The first televised presidential debates help tip the election to John F. Kennedy over Richard M. Nixon.

1961

- Backed by the CIA, Cuban exiles attempt a disastrous invasion of Cuba at the Bay of Pigs.

- A bus carrying "Freedom Riders" who seek to integrate the South is attacked and burned by whites in Anniston and Birmingham, Alabama.

▼ The Soviet Union and East Germany construct a wall in Berlin cutting off access to the western section of the city.

- The first U.S. suborbital space flight by Alan Shepard is launched by a Chrysler-built Mercury-Redstone rocket.

Sixties Firsts

In the 1960s, not a decade especially known for innovation in American automobiles, two Chrysler "firsts" stand out as remarkable, one which took, one which didn't. The first proved immensely practical. Since the beginning, most U.S. automobiles had received their electrical power from a DC generator. But generators were unable to generate energy at low engine speeds such as when a car was idling. As demands on a car's electrical system grew throughout the 1950s, the drawback proved ever more irksome. Alternators had seen limited use in taxis

Chrysler engineers perfected alternators, with greater efficiency at lower speeds, and introduced them on the 1960 Valiant to meet the increasing demands on a car's electrical system. Replacing generators used in almost all cars before the 1960s, this Chrysler "industry first" was soon adopted as standard equipment throughout the U.S. automobile industry.

and police cars, but they were big, cumbersome and expensive. Chrysler began work on an alternator that would be as cheap as a generator and about the same size. In 1960, the Company introduced the first practical, general-use alternator on the Valiant, and soon it was standard on all models.

The tale of Chrysler's turbine technology was not so sanguine. Chrysler began working with turbines in the late 1940s, when it developed a turboprop engine for the U.S. Navy. Chrysler installed a turbine in a Plymouth in 1954, and two years later, a turbine-powered Plymouth went from New York to the West Coast. The advantages

of a turbine engine were its quiet operation (although it sounded like a jet when powering up), its incredibly smooth, vibration-free drive and its low-end power. Its only negatives seemed fuel economy—at 11.5 mpg it was a gas guzzler—and turbo lag when accelerating. In 1961, Chrysler showcased a third-generation turbine and, in 1962, held customer-reaction tours of two turbine cars. Afterward, the Company announced it would build 75 turbines for customer testing but later reduced the number to 50 cars to be shared by 200 customers.

The program began in the fall of 1962. Despite the handsome, space-age styling of the Ghia-built bodies, which some said looked very much like Ford's Thunderbird, and near flawless performance for the evaluators, the test drivers complained—as Chrysler expected—about fuel economy, and a full third of them disliked the lag in acceleration. They did like, however, the styling and the silky ride. In the long run, problems with fuel economy, the lack of electronic control systems, and the unknowns of safety and emission standards looming on the horizon inhibited its further development. Today only a few collectors and museum curators ever experience the thrill of the Jet Age whine when the Chrysler turbine powers up.

In the 1960s, Chrysler built 50 of these stylish turbine cars for testing by 200 customers. They never entered general production.

1962

- The Soviet Union and the United States reach the brink of nuclear war over Soviet missiles deployed covertly in Cuba.

- U.S. marshals and 3,000 soldiers suppress riots when James Meredith arrives to begin classes as the first black man at the University of Mississippi.

- Kaiser Jeep introduces the Wagoneer for the 1963 model year. 1962 is the last year that the name Willys is used on Jeep vehicles.

- Biologist Rachel Carson publishes *Silent Spring*, a book whose description of an earth ravaged by pesticides kicks of the modern environmental movement.

- George Romney resigns from American Motors presidency to become governor of Michigan.

- Andy Warhol launches the Pop Art movement when he exhibits a large, beautifully silkscreened image of a can of Campbell's soup at New York's Stable Gallery.

- Chrysler produces 50 test cars powered by a turbine engine.

1963

- Betty Friedan publishes *The Feminine Mystique*, heralding a new wave of radical feminism.

- Chrysler Corporation introduces a five-year, 50,000-mile warranty.

- A stock-bodied Plymouth sedan sets a record at Bonneville: 196 mph.

▲ Martin Luther King addresses some 250,000 rallying in support of civil rights in a March on Washington.

■ The entire American Motors line is named "Car of the Year" by *Motor Trend Magazine*.

■ Chevrolet makes over the Corvette sports car into the Sting Ray, which represents a landmark in American sports car design.

■ Willys Motors becomes Kaiser Jeep.

■ President John F. Kennedy is assassinated in Dallas, Texas.

1964

■ The U.S. Surgeon General warns Americans that smoking cigarettes is dangerous to their health.

■ Chrysler buys a share in the British Rootes Group and controlling interest in SIMCA.

Design Muscle

When Elwood Engel came from Ford Motor Company to succeed Virgil Exner as head of Chrysler's Styling section, his assignment was to bring new models "back in the mainstream." His reputation was based on the beautiful 1961 Lincoln Continental, his signature car at Ford, and he used his previous work to inspire Chrysler's 1964 model line, from the Thunderbirdésque Chrysler Turbine to the Lincoln look-alike 1964 Imperial to the circa 1960 Ford-imitating 1965 Chrysler.

At first, the conservative look fostered by the new vice president of Styling consisted mainly of "filling out the corners of the box" in cars with straight sides and crisp lines, but he was flexible enough to change when he realized the "razor-edge" look was not what customers wanted. Gradually, Engel's models evolved to include aircraft-inspired touches such as the cockpit-style interiors and sweeping outward curves of the "fuselage" look. Perhaps the most memorable car of the Engel era, the 1968 Dodge Charger—with its intersecting "double diamond" front fender and door and diamond shapes on its quarter panels—was the Corporation's most original post-Exner statement. But

Brought from Ford in 1963 to guide Chrysler design back into the mainstream, Elwood Engel first concentrated on the conservative look he had ridden to success with the 1961 Lincoln Continental.

The styling of the early Engel era consisted of "filling out the corners of the box" with straight sides and crisp lines. Engel also developed the "fuselage" look as in this 1970 Chrysler Hurst.

the Coronet and Satellite coupes, especially the Super Bees and Road Runners, also still excite automobile buffs. Engel's later models packed high-performance engines under their hoods, which soon earned them the tag of "muscle cars." The new power along with the 1970 E-bodies of the Barracudas and Challengers and the flowing redesign of the Charger and Plymouth intermediates in 1971 created some of the most desirable "collectibles" in the short-lived muscle car era.

Engel's tenure at Chrysler, which came to a close with his retirement in 1972, completed the transition of the old, often neglected Styling section to a full-fledged design department, which brought the Corporation in line with the other Big Three automakers. After moving that year into the huge new Walter P. Chrysler Building, the department's name was changed from Styling to Design. Looming behind the name change was an attempt to reflect the multi-talented and more powerful role of the contemporary designer—part stylist, part engineer, part product planner, part manufacturing specialist. As a descriptive term, "styling" (still used occasionally and derisively) was tarnished in some minds by its associations with the chrome and fin excesses of the 1950s.

Boldness in the muscle car era came in colors rather than chrome. The Plymouth GTX (left), big brother of the Road Runner, was offered in a wide variety of vibrant hues, with names to match—Lime Light, Lemon Twist and Vitamin C Orange. The colors were accented with bold, wide stripes.

When Engel's models did break out of the box, they came with a hulking, animal-like pose, an optional air cleaner installed through the hood and a growling engine. Only 1,000 1970 Dodge Challenger T/As like this one were built for the street. Several V-8s—the 318, 340, 383, 440 Wedge and the 426 Hemi—were available.

1964

- Pontiac introduces the Tempest GTO, designed for power and performance, and kicks off the muscle car era.

- ▲ The Barracuda is introduced, beating the Ford Mustang (above) by two weeks into what becomes known as the "pony car" segment of the market.

- Congress passes the Civil Rights Act outlawing racial discrimination in all public places; it is the first of a series of legislative acts, including Medicare, aimed at creating the "Great Society" promoted by President Lyndon Johnson.

- Richard Petty, driving a Hemi-powered Plymouth, takes first place at the Daytona 500. Second and third places also go to Plymouths with Hemis.

- ▲ Three young members of the Congress on Racial Equality (CORE)—Mickey Schwerner, James Chaney and Andrew Goodman—are murdered in Mississippi for trying to register blacks to vote.

1964

■ Congress passes the Gulf of Tonkin Resolution, giving the president virtually a free hand in pursuing the growing conflict in Vietnam.

■ A popular British singing group, the Beatles, begin their first performing tour of the United States.

1965

▲ Ralph Nader publishes *Unsafe at Any Speed: The Designed-in Dangers of the American Automobile*, giving birth to the consumers' rights movement.

■ The controversial and highly influential African American activist Malcolm X is assassinated by three Black Muslims while speaking to a Harlem audience.

▲ Cesar Chavez, leader of the migrant farm workers in their strike against California growers, calls for a national boycott of table grapes.

Heyday of the Muscle Car

From the mid-1960s to the early 1970s, Americans, especially American males, fell in love with performance. No longer were young drivers content to get their thrills vicariously at the stock car races, where Richard Petty rode his Hemi-engine Plymouths to victory after victory. They wanted to take the experience home with them. And they did, as the Big Three began installing power plants from their larger cars in their intermediate and compact lines, creating a new market and a new subculture. The era of the muscle car was born.

The marketing of performance automobiles actually had its beginnings around 1955, when Chrysler introduced its Hemi engine with the 300 series and the following year debuted the Plymouth Fury and Dodge D-500. Ignoring those who thought of automobiles as mere transportation, Chrysler directed its relatively expensive but civilized 300 sport coupes at car enthusiasts who loved not only getting from point A to point B, but getting there fast. Chevrolet tested the waters in the performance market by promoting an option for increased power through a simple check-off box on the dealer order sheet. From these two developments grew a great

The sporty Barracuda was introduced in mid-1964. By 1965, the year of this model, buyers could purchase a "Formula S" package that included tightened suspension and a hotter engine.

By 1970, the ultimate 'Cudas, like the one below, boasted a Hemi under the hood.

rivalry between the auto companies for pushing power.

The trend was intertwined with the growing popularity of stock car racing. In 1965, Chrysler was forced to suspend its NASCAR activities because the organization declared that at least 1,000 engines had to be produced for street use for the engine type to be used in racing, which essentially outlawed the racing version of the 426 Hemi. Chrysler returned to the NASCAR circuit in 1966, after it built a street version of the 426, and won 111 of 131 major stock car races and set 80 new records on the five major circuits. On the street, versions of the Dodge and Plymouth muscle cars grew ever more powerful.

Word of mouth about this or that muscle car's capabilities moved down the streets faster than the cars themselves. Hot rod magazines proliferated. The Beach Boys sang songs about the cars their listeners loved. Owners spent weekends waxing and polishing their machines and dreamed of pulling up to stoplights and challenging other drivers off the line who had spent their weekends waxing and polishing their machines. Gas was cheap, the muscle cars affordable, and the summers seemingly endless. Then insurance rates soared, and the Organization of Petroleum Producing Countries (OPEC) shut off the tap in 1973. The era of cheap gas withered away.

CAR OF THE YEAR

The road runner bird was not the only cartoon used to promote Chrysler's muscle cars. The autos themselves became cartoons in Company ads.

In 1968, Plymouth introduced its budget muscle car, the Road Runner, which carried the famous cartoon road runner bird mascot and came with a horn that went "beep-beep" as standard equipment. A 1969 model is shown above.

Plymouth's Duster, like this 1970 Duster 340, became popular during the muscle car period.

Not only the Big Three, but also American Motors (premerger) produced muscle cars, like this 1968 AMX.

1965

■ Congress passes the Vehicle Air Pollution and Control Act, for the first time mandating that automakers change their products to meet nationwide pollution standards on 1968 models.

■ Martin Luther King leads a civil rights march on Selma, Alabama, where marchers are brutally beaten by a white mob.

■ Congress declares draft-card burning illegal.

1966

■ The U.S. Supreme Court rules in *Miranda v. State of Arizona* that the Constitution's 5th Amendment, allowing a defendant to refuse to testify in court on the grounds that such testimony might be self-incriminating, also extends to individuals in police custody.

■ The National Organization of Women is founded to lobby for liberalized abortion laws and an Equal Rights Amendment for women.

▲ The Black Panther Party is formed in Oakland, California.

■ Congress passes the Motor Vehicles Act, mandating the use of seat belts and the introduction of other safety measures by the automobile industry.

At the Track

In 1964, Ronnie Householder, a well-known race car driver working at Chrysler since he was hired to assist in the development of the early Plymouth Fury, became head of the Company's racing program. That same year, Chrysler introduced the 426 Hemi, often called the ultimate stock car engine. Richard Petty rode it to victory at the Daytona 500, while Plymouths driven by Jimmy Purdue and Paul Goldsmith came in second and third. Also in 1964, Petty drove on to the NASCAR title, winning nine races and finishing in the top five 28 more times.

Ford, trying to catch the juggernaut, announced plans to build a 427 cu. in. overhead cam engine, and NASCAR put its foot down. "Grand National racing is not a division for exotic hand-built racing engines," a spokesman declared. NASCAR invoked its 1,000-engine rule: at least 1,000 engines had to be produced for street use for the engine type to be used in racing. Consequently, in 1965, Chrysler suspended its corporate NASCAR activities while it developed Hemi engines for production cars consumers could afford. Petty again drove a Plymouth to the NASCAR title in 1967, at one point winning 10 races in a row.

Racing to victory after victory in his Number 43 Plymouths (far left), Richard Petty established a mystique that was at its height in the mid-1960s. Chrysler was happy to take advantage of that mystique in ads such as this one.

Dick Branster's and Roger Lindamood's "Color Me Gone" drag car became the "Top Stock Eliminator" at the National Hot Rod Association Nationals. The 1964 Dodge had an altered wheelbase, lightweight components and a 426 cu. in. Hemi engine.

"The Hemi was so superior to anything I'd ever driven before. It's got pure, brute horsepower. It's just a thrill to drive behind one."

—RICHARD PETTY

In 1969, Chrysler-backed teams—which had started the year with standard body styles—startled the stock car racing world with the introduction of the Dodge Daytona and the Plymouth Superbird. The basic idea for these new models came from Bob Rodger, father of the Chrysler 300. Chrysler developed the idea to produce cars with streamlined pointed noses, scooped front spoilers and 58-in. rear wings mounted 23 in. up the slip stream. They helped Chrysler dominate NASCAR racing in the late 1960s. Not just Petty, but drivers such as Charlie Gloztbach, Richard Brickhouse, Jim Vandiver, Ramo Stott, Bobby Issac (who won the 1969 NASCAR title) and Dick Brooks made the era a golden one for Chrysler racing. Ten of the first 13 cars in the 1970 Daytona 500 were Superbirds or Daytonas, including the Plymouth Pete Hamilton drove to victory. By season's end, Issac had taken the title again, this time with 11 wins and 21 top-five finishes. Petty, who finished fourth, picked up 18 victories in 40 starts.

NASCAR was not about to let this continue. In 1971, it limited the cars to 305 cu. in. engines and insisted on a carburetor restrictor plate that, still in use today, effectively put an end to the Hemi's reign over the NASCAR speedways.

The startlingly new pointed noses, scooped spoilers and rear wings of Daytonas and Superbirds were like nothing ever seen before on the race track.

The Dodge Charger Daytona, its design refined by testing its aerodynamics in a wind tunnel, became the first American production car to break 200 mph. A 1970 Charger gained fame as "General Lee" on the Dukes of Hazzard television program. Shown here is a 1969 Daytona model.

- Anti-Vietnam War protesters clash with Chicago Mayor Richard Daley's police force during the Democratic National Convention.

- Former Ford chief executive Robert McNamara resigns as secretary of defense after the stunning and coordinated attack by the Viet Cong in the TET Offensive explodes the myth that the U.S. is winning in Vietnam.

▲ Astronauts Neil Armstrong and Edwin "Buzz" Aldrin become the first humans to walk on the moon.

- For the first time, "fuselage styling" distinguishes the Dodge Charger Daytona, the Plymouth Road Runner and the Dodge SuperBee.

- Sony Corporation introduces the first videocassette, the Betamax.

▼ Some 400,000 young people gather on Max Yagur's farm near Woodstock, New York, for a three-day rock-and-roll concert celebrating peace, love and understanding.

Less Is More

THE SOCIAL UPHEAVAL of the 1960s took its toll in the 1970s. President Richard Nixon, under growing pressure from the establishment as well as radical protesters, brought the Vietnam War to a close by withdrawing U.S. troops and abandoning the never quite legitimate government of South Vietnam to its own devices. But the war failed to end quickly enough to save either his presidency or the American economy. In the wake of the "Pentagon Papers," which revealed the clandestine machinations of a political elite determined to carry on the war behind the back of the American people, Nixon withdrew into the White House as if it were a bunker. The administration formed illegal teams of political operatives to plug leaks, such as those that led to the publication of the secret papers in the *New York Times,* and to carry out covert "missions" against the Democrats and people Nixon considered his domestic enemies. The break-in at Watergate was only one such mission, but its going awry ultimately led to Congressional hearings, impeachment and Nixon's resignation.

The malaise at the center of government was only one aspect of the war's impact on American life. Lyndon Johnson's Great Society programs were bled dry by the costs of the conflict, and their promise of social equality and an end to poverty had died along with American soldiers in the rice paddies of Southeast Asia. Now the inflationary pressures of 10 years of ever more expansive fighting threatened the good life at home. Not only was 1971 the year Nixon bombed Cambodia, students protested the bombing in massive demonstrations that shut down college campuses across the nation, and the National Guard gunned down four protesters at Kent State University. It was also the year the president ordered a freeze on wages and prices and introduced other draconian measures designed to curb inflation and redress the country's rapidly deteriorating balance of payments. Even as a U.S. jury found Lt. William Calley guilty of murder for following orders during the My Lai massacre, Japan and several European nations revalued their currencies upward and the United States devalued the dollar twice, taking it off the gold standard. American business turned against the war, and Congress cut off its funding. In short, to the bitterness of the 1960's political struggles were now added the uncertainties of economic hard times, and even before OPEC announced an embargo on oil in 1973, many had the sense that matters had spun out of control.

The feeling would have its effect on the automobile industry. In the early 1970s, Detroit had reentered the low-end of the market to compete with foreign imports by producing subcompacts such as the Ford Pinto, the GM Vega, and the American Motors Gremlin. By 1973, due in part to the worldwide inflation and the two devaluations of the dollar, which drove up the price of imports, domestic small cars were selling well. But large and intermediate-size cars continued to be the industry's bread and butter. Engine-driven accessories such as air conditioners and the inhibiting effect of pollution controls on engine efficiency had made such cars, never very fuel efficient, gas guzzlers. GM's cars averaged 12 miles a gallon, Ford's and Chrysler's were not much better, and altogether they set a new postwar low in fuel economy. At the same time, Detroit—suffering like all American business from inflation, rising labor costs and the expense of regulation—was reluctant to take advantage of the technology that had made imports more efficient. None of this had been so critical when oil was cheap and plentiful and sacrificing a few gallons for a catalytic converter made sense, but by the summer of 1973, there were sporadic but ominous gasoline shortages at the pump. Then in October, the petroleum-exporting states of the Middle East, source of a 10th of the nation's oil supply, resorted to "oil diplomacy" in their conflict with Israel and declared an embargo on shipments of their product to Israel's ally, the United States.

The Arab oil embargo lasted half a year, during which period the government responded by declaring year-round Daylight Savings Time (quickly repealed) and a 55-mile-per-hour national speed limit to save fuel. Gasoline prices nevertheless shot up 30 percent, and in some places around the country, especially in the Northeast, service stations became clogged with long lines of cantankerous motorists. Skeptics later pointed out that the embargo was a chimera—as many as 700,000 barrels of Arab oil a day "leaked" into the United States, and three weeks before the Arabs lifted their embargo, oil stocks were 5 percent higher than in early 1973. There was some public outrage, and a few charged that the big oil companies had conspired to raise prices and drive independent operators out of business. Whatever the truth, the embargo threw Detroit into a tailspin. Car sales—especially those of larger automobiles—plummeted, and the nation tumbled into a deep recession. By 1975, automobile sales had dropped 38 percent below 1973's record level, the sharpest decline since the Great Depression. More than a quarter million auto workers lost their jobs. Chrysler suffered a 1975 loss of $259.5 million, the worst in automobile history. Many doubted the nation's number three auto company had much of a future.

Although the auto industry rebounded in 1976, the OPEC embargo made the public more aware of the statistics that environmentalists and other critics, especially in government, had been citing all along. America's dependence on foreign oil was growing, having reached 40 percent by 1976. Nearly a third of the petroleum products purchased by Americans annually were consumed by passenger cars. There were 106 mil-

GIs returning from Vietnam pass through a crowd of peace demonstrators in Seattle.

lion cars on the road in 1975, racking up well over a trillion miles. Early that year, concerned auto executives from GM, Ford and Chrysler pledged to create a voluntary program to increase fuel efficiency by 40 percent in five years. In response, consumer advocates pointed out what they considered Detroit's foot-dragging on pollution control and safety issues in recent times, and by 1978, Congress had introduced legislation to ensure that the industry met certain fuel efficiency goals. The Corporate Average Fuel Economy Act (CAFE) set fleet-wide mileage-per-gallon standards for American automakers.

In retrospect, then, 1973 was remembered as the beginning of the end for the big car in America, a passing hailed by many as an advance, bemoaned by others as the loss of a golden age, of a certain expansiveness and confidence. Clearly, for the first time since the Depression, average Americans had a taste of what it was like to *want*, to do without, and the catch phrase of the decade became "less is more." For some, Detroit's story was emblematic of the times. Suffering from confusion and mixed purposes, a once indomitable industry struggled to come to terms with domestic change and foreign challenge. The same could be said of an America beset in turn by the Watergate Crisis, the Energy Crisis, and now the Iran Hostage Crisis. But neither condition was permanent, and the mid-1980s would see a return to prosperity that surprised nay-sayers and defenders alike. In the long run, one of the more permanent effects of the economic entrenchment of the 1970s was to create a real market for smaller, more fuel-efficient cars, which in turn offered Chrysler Corporation, which had been pushed to the wall, an opportunity to reinvent itself. And it did.

▲ National guardsmen fire
into a crowd of Kent State
University students
protesting the war in
Vietnam, killing four and
wounding nine.

■ AMC Gremlin becomes the
first U.S. subcompact since
the early 1950s.

■ American Motors acquires
Jeep and makes it the Jeep
Corporation, a subsidiary
of AMC.

▲ Congress passes the Clean
Air Act, which mandates a
90 percent reduction in
auto emission pollutants
within six years.

1971

■ To check raging inflation
and strengthen the U.S.
trade imbalance, President
Richard Nixon imposes a
freeze on wages and prices,
then devalues the dollar.
Japan and Europe revalue
their currencies upward.

■ The federal government
bans cigarette advertising
on television.

■ Chrysler begins marketing
Dodge Colts, produced by
Mitsubishi.

Crisis in the Seventies

By the mid-1970s, events were conspiring to make big American cars like the Chryslers of the late 1960s and early 1970s the dinosaurs of the automobile industry. In late 1973, the mostly Middle Eastern countries of the Organization of Petroleum Exporting Companies (OPEC) declared an embargo on oil exports to nations that had supported Israel in its war against Egypt, and Americans soon found themselves waiting in line at the filling station to purchase gas at much inflated prices. Congress reduced the national speed limit to 55 miles per hour in 1974 in order to conserve gas, marking the end of a muscle car era already fast fading under the impact of smaller, cheaper, more fuel-efficient imports from Western Europe and Japan. The following year, Congress passed the Corporate Average Fuel Economy (CAFE) Act, setting for a manufacturer's collective product fleet-wide gas mileage targets, which began to go into effect in 1978. When Americans were taken hostage by Islamic revolutionaries in Iran in 1979, the United States embargoed Iranian oil, tightening supplies and sending gas prices even higher.

Although Chrysler had begun marketing small auto-

The Arab oil embargo, beginning in October 1973, triggered an energy crisis in the United States, Western Europe and Japan—a crisis that struck the American automobile industry particularly hard. By February 1974, long gas lines like this one were commonplace.

mobiles built by Mitsubishi under the Dodge Colt name, it—like the rest of the American automobile industry—was caught short by these events. In 1975, changing its long-standing policy of producing no "junior edition" Chryslers, the Company introduced the Cordoba, which advertising pitch man Ricardo Montalban made famous for its "rich Corinthian leather." The smallest postwar Chrysler yet, the Cordoba represented the Company's attempt to penetrate the market for "personal" size coupes. Instantly popular with the buying public, the Cordoba garnered 60 percent of sales in 1975 and encouraged the Company in its new "less is more" direction.

In 1978, Chrysler introduced the mid-size LeBaron and the first U.S. subcompacts, the Dodge Omni and the Plymouth Horizon; in 1979, it promoted a smaller New Yorker for both style and economy. The rebates and buyer incentives offered in advertisements focusing on fuel economy and sales price hinted at the hard times that the American automobile industry in general, and Chrysler in particular, were suffering. Despite the success of the Cordoba, the Dodge Aspen and the Plymouth Volaré, which Chrysler touted as small cars "with the accent on comfort," Chrysler ended the decade in financial trouble that left many doubting the Company would survive.

The best-known feature of the Cordoba was probably the "rich Corinthian leather" with which most came outfitted. The phrase passed into the lexicon of American automobile history courtesy of one of the more famous advertising campaigns ever mounted, featuring Ricardo Montalban, who stands here beside the car in a pose familiar from thousands of television spots and magazine pages. When asked "where does Corinthian leather come from?" a Chrysler spokesperson responded, "Corinth."

Introduced in 1975, the Cordoba was an instant hit. The shortest model in decades—just 2.5 in. longer than a 1924 Chrysler Six—Cordobas like this 1976 model were "personal" size coupes on a 115-in. wheelbase with Jaguar-like front-end styling cues, featuring chrome grilles and individual headlamp and parking-lamp forms, formal roofs and subtle "blister" fender contours.

1971

- The *New York Times* launches a series of articles called collectively the "Pentagon Papers" and based on a secret government study of U.S. involvement in Vietnam.

1972

- President Nixon and Soviet Secretary-General Leonid Brezhnev announce a policy of *détente*, relaxing Cold War tensions.

▲ Nixon become the first U.S. president to visit Communist China.

- Five employees of the Nixon campaign's Committee to Re-elect the President are caught burglarizing the Democratic National Committee's headquarters at the Watergate apartment complex.

▲ Palestinian terrorists belonging to the "Black September" group infiltrate the Olympic Village in Munich, killing two Israeli athletes and taking nine others hostage. A botched rescue ends in a shoot-out that leaves five of the eight terrorists and all the hostages dead.

- U.S. ground combat troops withdraw from Vietnam.

1973

- In *Roe v. Wade*, the U.S. Supreme Court rules that a woman has a constitutional right to privacy that includes the right to abort a fetus during the first trimester of pregnancy.

- Jeep introduces "Quadratrac"—or four-wheel drive.

▲ *The Godfather* wins the Academy Award for best picture.

- The Arab-controlled Organization of Petroleum Exporting Countries (OPEC) declares an embargo on oil exports to nations supporting Israel in the Yom Kippur War earlier in the year.

- Daimler-Benz's foreign sales outstrip its domestic sales, and the company begins making trucks in the United States.

- Chile's President Salvador Allende dies in a U.S.-backed military coup.

1974

- Worldwide inflation and an energy crisis caused by a shortage of oil create dramatic increases in the cost of fuel, food and raw materials. In most industrialized nations, economic growth slows to near zero.

- To save fuel, Congress imposes a 55 mile-per-hour speed limit nationwide.

- The Jeep Cherokee debuts.

Small Advances

In the 1970s, with the automobile industry increasingly beset by new competition from foreign imports and concern over the energy crisis growing, the struggling Chrysler Corporation turned to producing smaller, more sensible and sometimes safer cars. In 1971, the Company offered antilock brakes as a $250 option on its Imperials. Called the "Sure-Brake System," it featured a sensor on each wheel, an electronic controller and three vacuum power modulators. On the dash's instrument panel, the now familiar warning light signaled an automatic system check every time the engine was started and system failure whenever one occurred. Like today's ABS systems, Sure-Brake detected potential wheel lock-up and pulsed hydraulic pressure to the brakes. Although this pioneering braking system was offered for the next few years, safety equipment became popular only gradually over the course of two decades. Sure-Brake quietly slipped from the list of options due to adverse customer reaction to the system's noise and vibration.

Later in the decade, Chrysler launched the first U.S.-built subcompacts, the front-wheel-drive Dodge Omni and Plymouth Horizon. Introduced to meet a need, they

Scenes such as this of Japanese imports on the Boston docks drove the American automobile industry in a new direction in the 1970s.

were derived from the SIMCA 1100 produced in France by Chrysler's SIMCA affiliate, and they boasted some firsts. Almost all of today's front-wheel-drive cars have transversely mounted engines. Chrysler was the first American manufacturer to go with this design, installing the 1978 Omni and Horizon four-cylinder engines in the now typical east-west configuration. Also offered first on the Omnis and Horizons was a new convenience feature—the first 17-function, column-mounted control lever. The control lever, which put frequently used functions at the driver's fingertips, was a step forward in the kind of automobile ergonomics

the industry practices today almost as a matter of course.

In general, however, the 1970s were not years marked by new directions in Chrysler products. The well-documented financial troubles experienced by the Company in those years meant that there was little money to finance serious new innovations, and the financial struggles naturally affected employee morale. Instead, Chrysler would be forced to create something different out of what it had basically in hand in order to produce the small, conservative, economical cars it seemed at the time the public was coming to demand. The day of the K-Car was just beyond the horizon.

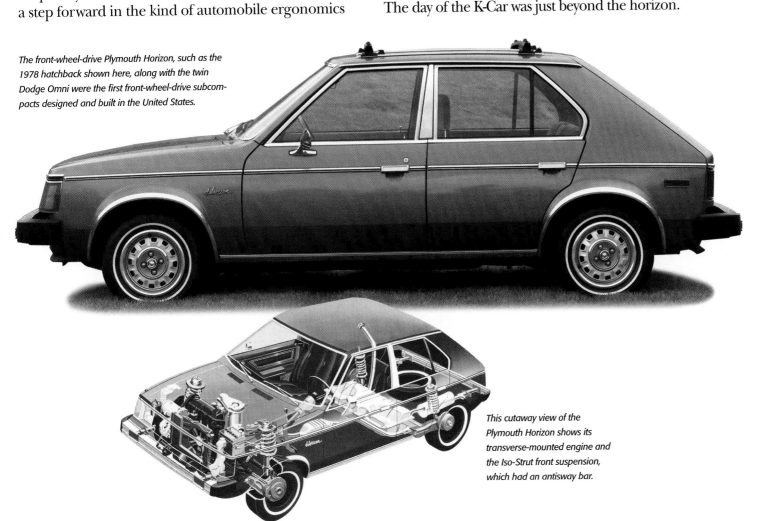

The front-wheel-drive Plymouth Horizon, such as the 1978 hatchback shown here, along with the twin Dodge Omni were the first front-wheel-drive subcompacts designed and built in the United States.

This cutaway view of the Plymouth Horizon shows its transverse-mounted engine and the Iso-Strut front suspension, which had an antisway bar.

1974

■ The Barracuda is discontinued.

▲ Under threat of impeachment, Richard Nixon resigns as president of the United States.

1975

■ *Popular Electronics* magazine and the MITS Company introduce a $400 build-it-yourself computer for hobbyists called the "Altair 8800," the first personal computer.

■ U.S. unemployment rate reaches 9.2 percent, the highest since the Great Depression ended in 1941.

▲ U.S. embassy personnel and the last remaining American forces evacuate Saigon hours before its fall to the advancing Vietnamese National Liberation Front army.

■ Chrysler introduces its first "junior-size" model–the Cordoba.

Loans and Labor

In serious financial straits during the 1970s, Chrysler Corporation sought and acquired U.S. government-backed loans in 1980. In 1978, Chrysler Chairman John Riccardo approached the Farmers Home Administration with a request for $250 million in loan guarantees, most of that earmarked for building a new factory in Richmond, Indiana. Despite Riccardo's extensive lobbying, the government denied the request. With sales slumping and cash running extremely low, Riccardo brought in Lee Iacocca, recently fired from Ford Motor Company, as president. Less than a year later, Riccardo resigned as board chairman, citing as one reason the possibility that his presence might "hinder the final passage" of loan guarantees that the Carter administration had already indicated it would support.

Chairman and CEO Iacocca then mounted a massive lobbying campaign with the help of new Chrysler President Gerald Greenwald and financial wizard Steve Miller. With help from the United Auto Workers, they worked both houses of Congress to obtain the loan guarantees, and four months later they got them. Under the Loan Guarantee Act of 1979, the government prom-

Retiring Chrysler Chairman John Riccardo tried and failed to get modest loan guarantees from the government for plant expansion before hiring Lee Iacocca.

One of Lee Iacocca's first hires was Gerald Greenwald, then working for Ford of Venezuela. Two years later, Greenwald became president of the Company and played a major role in putting together the loan guarantee package.

Recruited by Gerald Greenwald, Steve Miller was instrumental in negotiating and renegotiating Chrysler's loans with banks during the Congressional loan guarantee hearings.

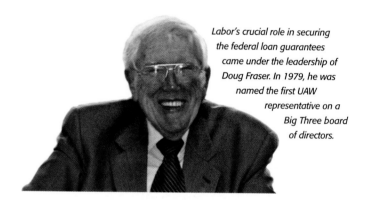

Labor's crucial role in securing the federal loan guarantees came under the leadership of Doug Fraser. In 1979, he was named the first UAW representative on a Big Three board of directors.

In seeking the federal loan guarantees, Lee Iacocca had trumpeted Chrysler as a truly American company, a theme the Corporation continued to emphasize in advertising its products afterward.

Chrysler technology makes Made in America mean something again.

ised to secure $1.5 billion in private-sector borrowing, provided Chrysler could renegotiate its extensive loans with lenders and gain union concessions. Struck by a barrage of criticism from the financial press, Iacocca and other Company officials pointed out that these were guarantees, not loans, and that not a single dollar of federal money would ever change hands.

Labor's role in the affair proved decisive for both the guarantees and for the early payback of the loans. The government had basically cosigned Chrysler's loans on the assumption that failing to do so would cost even more in unemployment and lost taxes if the Company went bankrupt and 800,000 to 1 million workers lost their jobs. Under the leadership of UAW President Doug Fraser, Chrysler's workers gave up billions of dollars in pension guarantees and wages to help the Company push its proposals through Congress. To effect these concessions, Fraser himself was elected to the board of directors, the first time in history a major labor leader was given a seat at management's table. With the backing of both labor and the federal government, Chrysler was able to launch new products under development, initially the K-Car and ultimately the first minivan, and turn the Company around.

The loan guarantee program allowed Chrysler to launch its successful K-Cars, which became a mainstay of the Corporation for years. The K-Car platform was the basis for the 1986 Chrysler LeBaron, a new version of the venerable Town & Country nameplate.

Lee Iacocca toasts Chrysler independence from U.S. government supervision of the Company's operations at a formal ceremony for the repayment of the final two-thirds of the federally guaranteed notes Chrysler borrowed from private investors in 1980. Effective August 15, 1983, seven years earlier than required under the Loan Guarantee Act of 1979, Chrysler Corporation retired its outstanding debt.

1978

■ Lesley Brown gives birth to a child conceived outside her womb through in vitro fertilization, the world's first "test-tube" baby.

■ Egyptian President Anwar Sadat and Israeli Prime Minister Menachem Begin sign a separate peace called the Camp David Accords.

■ Congress passes the Corporate Average Fuel Economy (CAFE) Act, setting fleet-wide mile-per-gallon standards for American automakers.

1979

■ Revolutionary Marxists called the Sandinistas oust Nicaraguan dictator Anastasio Somoza Debayle.

■ After a partial meltdown in the nuclear reactor at the Three Mile Island electric power plant near Harrisburg, Pennsylvania, releases radioactive gases into the atmosphere, officials close the plant and evacuate the island.

▲ After the Ayatollah Ruhollah Khomeini leads a successful revolution against the Shah of Iran, radical Islamic supporters take 90 Americans hostage.

■ Renault buys shares in AMC.

Morning in America

THE DECADE OF the 1980s began with the building of one wall—the Vietnam Memorial—and ended with the tearing down of another—the Berlin Wall. Both, in their own way came to represent the passing of an era, and both were followed by a surprising new direction in the affairs of the nation and the world.

Designed in 1981 by Yale undergraduate Maya Ying Lin, the Vietnam Memorial's somber black wall was—like almost everything about the war—controversial, at least at first. Critics felt that the radical "modern" design was somehow a statement about the war's pointlessness, and they were vociferous enough to get a traditional statue of three American foot soldiers added nearby. But from the moment the memorial opened, the wall—listing the names of all those killed in the fighting—became a national shrine and the most visited site in Washington, D.C. Thousands made rubbings of the names on the wall, touched them, kissed them. Many placed at the wall's base personal memorabilia, flowers, pictures, letters, even medals. In a myriad of individual outbursts of emotion, visitors engaged in what amounted to a national purging of the war's bitter legacy.

Ronald Reagan took the oath of office the year the memorial was dedicated, and he came to the White House promising a new dawn in America. Certainly one could see in Reagan's popularity a longing in Americans to put the sourness of the recent past behind them and a nostalgia for less complicated times. After Watergate, in the "stagflation" of the Jimmy Carter years and the national humiliation of the Iran hostage crisis, it seemed that the traditional American suspicion of authority had grown into wholesale cynicism about government. Reagan's revolution consisted of dismantling—via budget cuts—many of the vestiges of FDR's New Deal and Lyndon Johnson's Great Society and of the unleashing—with tax rebates and a decidedly pro-business agenda—of the bulls on Wall Street. Amid the din of the disco clubs and the buzz on the floor of the Stock Exchange, one could hear the echo of a different American past, something of the roar, say, of the 1920s. In the renewed feelings of prosperity and the unfettered ambitions of the cigar-smoking young urban professionals, one could catch a glimpse of their grandfathers who had trod sure afoot the well-manicured suburban lawns of the 1950s.

Chrysler, too, shared in the prosperity of the mid-1980s. It began the decade bleakly enough, nearly bankrupt and out of touch with customers that now found wire wheels and landau irons corny. With a federal loan guarantee and major concessions from the auto workers, the Company bought time for its engineers to create a new kind of car. The K-Cars, however boxy and awkward they might look today, held their own among the smaller, four- and six-cylinder, front-wheel-drive, quality-conscious Japanese imports that were swamping the market. Healthy sales allowed the Company to bring back the virtually extinct convertible and to produce the first minivan, both with great success. Profits from this truly unique vehicle made it possible for Chrysler to join in the new merger mania

The two men who shaped the end of the Cold War: Ronald Reagan and Mikhail Gorbachev.

1985 in a Russia that Reagan labeled the "Evil Empire" and at a time when Cold War tensions were higher than they had been since the early 1960s. Faced with the need to spend prodigiously on defense in order to compete with Reagan's "Star Wars" initiative, the Soviet Union plunged into economic and social crisis. In order to fix the problems, the new premier broke with hard-line Communist party members and introduced a series of reforms, falling under the general categories of *perestroika* (restructuring) and *glasnost* (openness). These ultimately led to the deterioration of Communist control in Eastern Europe and the collapse of the Soviet Union itself. Allowing for the real differences in circumstance, Gorbachev in effect shared much the same philosophical foundation as Reagan, who had been reelected to the presidency by a landslide in 1984. Both men opposed "statism," whether of the deadly vicious kind practiced by Joseph Stalin or the more benign version that formed FDR's legacy, and both men championed the spirit of individualism. As a result, by 1989, communism was spent and capitalism refreshed, the forces of totalitarianism in retreat and those of democracy on the rise. The building of the Berlin Wall at the height of the Cold War in 1961 now seemed an empty gesture, surely one that had outlived its usefulness.

As the Wall tumbled, the Cold War came to an end. Suddenly, the reckless national security system it had engendered—in which two superpowers, armed with weapons capable of destroying the planet many times over, divided the world into hostile camps, vied for influence over nonaligned Third World countries and held each other in check at tremendous cost to their own people in terms of both riches and freedom—seemed superfluous. But in its wake, the Cold

of the period and purchase—among other companies—American Motors from its French partner, Renault. AMC not only provided Chrysler with the premier four-wheel-drive vehicle, the Jeep, at precisely the time four-wheel drive was going from the odd to the virtually compulsory, it also brought new blood into management just as the turnaround of the 1980s began to fizzle. Nevertheless, it was a remarkable turnaround, one that rivaled, in the annals of automotive history, the most significant story of the late 20th century: the near-complete disappearance of communism.

Mikhail Gorbachev was Ronald Reagan's counterpart in the Communist world. He came to power in

War left a murkier world. The United States was massively in debt from the soaring deficits encouraged by Reagan's ambitious defense spending. Its inner cities were deeply troubled, with the epidemic of AIDS and illicit drugs underscoring the deepening gap between the country's rich and poor. Critics pointed to the 1986 Iran-Contra scandal, which recalled the embarrassments of Watergate, as an even more dangerous abuse of power than that demonstrated by the Nixon White House. The 1987 stock market crash, the first since 1929, looked to many like the comeuppance that the wildly successful investment bankers (yuppies so young they thought the market only went up) so richly deserved. Those same critics enjoyed the insider trading scandals that brought down two of Wall Street's most arrogant billionaires—Ivan Boesky and Michael Millkin. The growing number of homeless were reminiscent of the Hoovervilles that had followed the collapse of the Republican prosperity of the 1920s. When Vice President George Bush, about to replace Reagan in the White House, felt the need to promise a "kinder, gentler nation" than his congenial boss had created, it was clear that Americans felt ambivalent about their Cold War "victory."

Indeed, some wits noted, the Cold War was over, and Japan had won. Certainly, the imported products of the Asian economic giant were everywhere evident. Americans drove Nissans, Toyotas and Hondas, listened to rap music on Sony Walkman equipment, dropped digitally remixed jazz and rock-and-roll into Japanese-made CD players and flipped to MASH and Miami Vice on big-screen Japanese-made television sets. Eventually, however, the Iran-Contra hearings came to a close, hardly denting Ronald Reagan's legacy; the stock market shook off its fall and began

another remarkable climb; criminal traders went to jail or made their plea bargains and returned to society; and the country continued to tilt right, giddy with the sense of a new beginning. The Japanese might buy Rockefeller Center or an American movie studio, but they were also opening shop and paying taxes in the United States. At least the country had not collapsed like its erstwhile foe, the Soviet Union, and there was still time, Americans seemed to feel, for its traditionally restless people to do what they probably did best—improvise. At Chrysler, too, improvising was becoming a way of doing business, as a new breed—some having studied Japanese business methods, others having learned at the lean AMC training ground—began tearing down their own walls and working in what they called "platform teams."

The go-go 1980s were not prosperous for everyone. Here, in 1985, an 11-year-old boy sleeps in his homeless family's car.

▲ Ted Turner launches the Cable News Network (CNN), the world's first 24-hour all-news television channel.

■ AMC introduces the Eagle, the first major four-wheel-drive passenger car of the modern car era in the United States.

■ The labor union Solidarity strikes the shipyards in Gdansk, Poland, beginning a process that will bring down Communist party rule and crack open the Iron Curtain.

■ Iraq goes to war with Iran.

■ Congress passes the Loan Guarantee Act, providing security for Chrysler to borrow from private lenders.

▼ President Jimmy Carter breaks off diplomatic relations with Iran over Americans it holds hostage and mounts an ill-fated commando raid to rescue them. When it fails utterly, Secretary of State Cyrus Vance resigns in protest.

K-Car Comeback

By the early 1980s, Chrysler was in dire financial troubles. Dedicated to full-size automobiles and muscle cars, the Company was caught short by the energy crisis and by the car-buying public's turn to smaller, more fuel-efficient imports. While new Chairman Lee Iacocca, with considerable help from the United Auto Workers, fought for Chrysler's very life on Wall Street and in Washington, Chrysler's Engineering and Design staff worked on a front-wheel-drive car that they hoped would rescue the

Company. Drawing on the clever employment of technology at hand, they used a bit of engineering legerdemain to create in 1981 a "survival" car whose designation within the Company—the K-Car—became so emblematic of Chrysler's new direction that it migrated to the nameplate of the vehicle itself.

Compact and functional, the car was relentlessly rectangular, and designers dubbed the clay model covered in maroon Di-Noc "the metal brick." The finished K-Car was nevertheless precisely the product the public wanted at the time—small, conservative, inexpensive and economical. The car had a new 2.2-

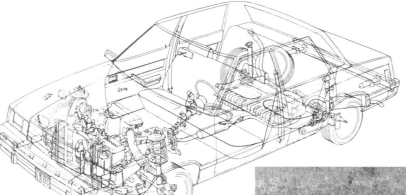

Front-wheel drive, used by Chrysler on the Plymouth Horizon, was carried forward to the K-Car platform, which not only helped lead Chrysler back from the brink of bankruptcy but served as the basis for generations of Chrysler models that followed.

"The K-Car was the last train from the station. If we failed here, it was all over."

—LEE IACOCCA

liter overhead cam four-cylinder engine with hemispherical combustion chambers, a unit-body chassis, MacPherson struts, rack and pinion steering and front-disc/rear-drum brakes—nothing spectacularly new but an excellent use of limited resources that produced a car with unusual space efficiency. The K-Cars had to sell, and they did, helping to lead Chrysler back from the brink of bankruptcy.

Indeed, they played a dual role. On the one hand, K-Cars kept the Company afloat. On the other, they served as an economical base for a variety of products. Throughout the 1980s, Chrysler's designers and engineers kept the K-Car platform but ever more ingeniously transfigured the lowly original into a seemingly endless series of new cars. An E-body was followed by G-, H-, P-, A-, J-, C- and Y-bodies. There were some new model names (Lancer, Shadow and Acclaim) and some venerated (LeBaron, New Yorker and Imperial). But along with the 1983 introduction of the triumphant "Vehicle of the Decade," the minivan, the K-Car and its platform underpinned one of the more miraculous turnarounds not only in the history of the automobile industry but also in the history of corporate America.

Fuel efficiency became the main selling point in advertisements for the K-Cars, although warranties and rebates were also frequently highlighted.

Public acceptance of the K-Car twins, the Dodge Aries and the Plymouth Reliant, like the 1981 "red brick" shown here, helped save the Corporation. The K-Car played a central role in the five-year survival plan Chrysler executives presented to Congress in their work to secure government-backed loans.

Magic Wagon

The biggest engineering, design and sales achievement for Chrysler Corporation in the 1980s was the introduction in 1983 of the minivan, a triumph of the design mantra that form should follow function. Harold "Hal" Sperlich had watched the development of a minivan-type vehicle when he worked as a product planner for Lee Iacocca at Ford in the early 1970s. But the Mini-Max, as they called it, had flaws—its step-up was too high, the roof was not low enough to fit into a garage, and there was no "nose" in the front to house the engine and offer a crush cushion in case of accidents. Even after Sperlich addressed these issues, Henry Ford II was not in the mood to experiment, and the Mini-Max was shelved in the late 1970s.

Sperlich moved to Chrysler and later became vice president of Product Planning and Design. By the early 1980s, he began to champion Chrysler engineers' designs for a minivan for which development money had not been available. If the K-Car indicated that Chrysler still knew how to employ effective engineering, the minivan proved the Company could still be innovative. A startlingly new vehicle that drove and looked like a car but

The 1984 Plymouth Voyager was powered by either a 2.2-liter or 2.6-liter four-cylinder engine, with automatic or five-speed manual transmissions. Over the years, Chrysler added longer wheelbases on some models, V-6 engines, four-wheel drive, reclining seats, dual air bags, integrated child safety seats and side impact protection. In Europe, it even sold a diesel version. Shown here is the first Voyager, vehicle identification number LAI NO1 11283 (Lee Iacocca's initials, the number "1," and the date).

offered the space of a van, the minivan rocked the establishment and changed the face of the automobile industry. *Road & Track* praised "the sheer novelty of the vehicle," while *Car and Driver* called it "the only American-built van that's not a truck" and credited Sperlich for inventing it and Iacocca, who had moved from Ford to Chrysler in 1978, for creating a "quick-acting management team" to get it produced. As every automobile company selling cars in the United States raced to release its own version of a minivan, Chrysler dominated the new market for a decade with its Chrysler Town & Country, Dodge Caravan and Plymouth Voyager. Most credit the minivan

with enabling Chrysler to pay off all the loans guaranteed by the federal government well ahead of time.

The car was an unparalleled success. A decade after Chrysler introduced the minivan, it still accounted for nearly 50 percent of all sales, and its three nameplates accounted for more sales than the nation's top seller, the Ford F-150 pickup, and more than all the cars sold by Nissan. The dark days of the 1970s were over, and the new, financially secure Chrysler would soon begin to expand, purchasing companies such as American Motors and Lamborghini, while entering into joint ventures with companies such as Maserati and Mitsubishi.

Chrysler Chairman Lee Iacocca introduced the Company's new breed of "garageable" 1984 front-wheel-drive family wagons and vans, which the world soon came to call, generically, the "minivan."

The minivan was aimed, as Road & Track *put it, at "current station wagon owners: those who already own larger, less efficient club wagons; growing families; those who need station wagons but hate the stodgy suburban image; women who aren't comfortable driving large conventional vans; people who used to own full-size sedans and like plenty of interior room; and those who enjoy the sheer novelty of the vehicle," the kind of folks Chrysler shows climbing into a Dodge Grand Caravan in this ad.*

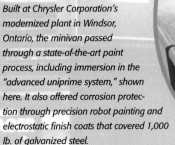

Built at Chrysler Corporation's modernized plant in Windsor, Ontario, the minivan passed through a state-of-the-art paint process, including immersion in the "advanced uniprime system," shown here. It also offered corrosion protection through precision robot painting and electrostatic finish coats that covered 1,000 lb. of galvanized steel.

1983

- President Ronald Reagan dubs the Soviet Union the "Evil Empire" and launches the Strategic Defense Initiative, nicknamed "Star Wars."

- Compact discs are marketed commercially for the first time.

- AMC-Renault introduces the Alliance.

- The National Science Foundation combines its computerized research lines (NSFNet) with the Defense Department's secure communications lines (the Advanced Research Projects Agency Network, or ARPANET), established in 1969, and creates a widely distributed network capable of handling far greater traffic, dubbed the "Internet."

- Chrysler pays off its guaranteed loans seven years ahead of schedule and introduces the minivan and the Shelby Charger.

1984

▼ Chrysler buys part of Maserati and introduces the Daytona and Laser sports coupes.

1984

- In one of history's worst industrial accidents, poison gas leaks from a Union Carbide plant in Bhopal, India, killing 2,500 and injuring some 200,000.

- AMC introduces the Jeep Cherokee, named "4 X 4 of the Year" by three off-road magazines.

- Three years after IBM began selling "home" or "personal" computers, Apple launches its user-friendly, mouse-driven microcomputer, the Macintosh, and the PC market explodes.

1985

- A crack cocaine epidemic spreads through the poorest inner-city neighborhoods across the United States.

- Soviet Premier Mikhail Gorbachev announces a program of *perestroika* ("restructuring") to rejuvenate the Soviet system by introducing free enterprise and normalized relations with the West and of *glasnost* ("openness") that includes the uncensored sharing of ideas and information.

- The U.S. officially becomes the world's largest debtor nation, with a $130 billion deficit.

Buying American

Chrysler's remarkably successful turnaround following the federal loan guarantee, the introduction of the K-Car and the launch of the minivan led the Corporation on a spending spree in the mid-1980s. The Company bought Gulfstream Aviation and Italy's Lamborghini while launching joint ventures with Maserati and Mitsubishi, but by far its most significant acquisition was American Motors in 1987.

Formed in 1954 out of Detroit's Hudson Motor Car Company and the Nash Motor Company (Nash-Kelvinator) of Kenosha, Wisconsin, American Motors had obtained the nearly defunct Kaiser Willys Sales Corporation in 1970 and, with it, the durable Jeep marque. Chronically underfunded and saddled with a weak dealer network, American Motors and its feisty Ramblers had seen some glory days under George Romney in the 1950s, but the company struggled throughout the next two decades until its purchase in 1979 by the venerable French automaker Renault. The most valuable asset in the AMC/Renault inventory was the Jeep, which maintained steady sales despite its aging Toledo factory and serious labor troubles. In 1984, AMC

During its heyday, AMC was perhaps best known to most as the maker of Ramblers. The first modern compact car, the Rambler (right) was introduced in 1950 by Nash-Kelvinator, whose merger with Hudson Motors in 1954 would create American Motors. Just before the merger, Nash-Kelvinator introduced another small car, the experimental Metropolitan, also called the NXI. Metropolitans were sold under the Nash, Hudson and AMC nameplates before the line was discontinued in 1962. The 1961 model shown above was one of 94,986 Metropolitans produced for AMC by Austin in England for sale in the United States and Canada.

produced its first small profit since 1979 with the introduction of an updated Jeep Cherokee and Jeep Wagoneer, but renewed labor difficulties the following year led to sabotage of the new Cherokees and soured relations to the breaking point. Renault had announced a $1 billion loss (although former AMC President Joe Cappy would claim that AMC itself was quite profitable before 1988) and was openly discussing the shut-down of the Toledo plant when Chrysler came along.

Jeep proved to be a gold mine for Chrysler, even if the other cars coming out of AMC and its descendant within the Company, the Jeep/Eagle Division, were suspect.

Although Chrysler President Robert Lutz later credited the Eagle Premier, a sedan introduced by Chrysler in 1987, as forming the basis for its successful LH cars in the 1990s, the real profit from the purchase of AMC came with its people. Accustomed to working in a freewheeling, close-to-the-bone style at AMC, folks such as Joe Cappy and engineer François Castaing became major champions of cross-functional teamwork at Chrysler while Steve Harris and Jim Julow assumed key positions in Chrysler public relations and marketing. In purchasing AMC, Chrysler got not only a new product line but a spunky spirit that would help to mold its future.

AMC's executives came to play a key role in the resurgence of Chrysler in the 1990s. Top engineer François Castaing, for example, came from Renault and American Motors to direct the conversion of car development at Chrysler to a platform team concept.

AMC's most valuable asset for Chrysler was the Jeep brand name. Chrysler continued to develop the line, and this 1993 Grand Cherokee was one of the earliest products of the Company's new cross-functional team approach. For the debut of the Grand Cherokee, President Bob Lutz introduced the first luxury sport-utility vehicle by crashing it through a showroom window at the Detroit Auto Show.

1986

▲ President Ronald Reagan admits to secretly trading arms for hostages in Iran in breach of the U.S. arms embargo, sparking the "Irangate" scandal, Congressional hearings and the indictment of Colonel Oliver North.

■ A nuclear reactor at Chernobyl, near the city of Kiev in the Soviet Union, explodes, sending a cloud of dangerous radioactive gas over the Ukraine and into parts of Europe.

■ AMC introduces the Jeep Wrangler.

■ The European Single Act paves the way for the elimination of all trade barriers among European nations and the creation of a single, unified European market.

▼ The space shuttle *Challenger* explodes on take-off.

1987

■ At the Montreal Conference, 24 nations call for eliminating the production of ozone-damaging chlorofluorocarbons (CFCs) used widely in aerosol sprays and air conditioners.

1987

- Chrysler buys AMC and AMC-Jeep from Renault; the Company also purchases Lamborghini.

- Gary Hart withdraws from the presidential race after reports of a sexual liaison with model Donna Rice, launching a new era of sensationalized news coverage of American politicians.

▲ Bill Gates, 32-year-old founder of Microsoft, becomes the microprocessing industry's first billionaire.

1988

- Palestinians in the Occupied Territories begin a prolonged resistance to Israeli rule called the "Intifada."

- Chrysler begins a joint venture with Mitsubishi called "Diamond Star."

- A U.S. medical survey concludes that aspirin, taken daily, cuts the risk of heart attack in half.

American (and European) Dreams

In the late 1980s, Chrysler created two noteworthy concept cars. The first came when Chrysler acquired Lamborghini in 1987. The purchase led Chrysler to produce a bold statement of the direction in which it intended to take the Italian automaker: the Lamborghini Portofino concept car. The basis for the Portofino was a concept car Chrysler had developed in 1986 called the Navajo, which had never gotten beyond the clay model stage. Chrysler renamed the new vehicle after a picturesque Italian seaport and introduced the automobile at the 1987 Frankfurt Auto Show. Built on the chassis of Lamborghini's mid-engine V-8 Jalpa, the Portofino was stretched by 66 cm to allow space for four seats. Chrysler fashioned the doors to mimic the forward-opening "scissor doors" of the 12-cylinder Countach, perhaps the best known of the Lamborghinis in this country. The rear doors pivoted backward in a similar fashion, thus eliminating the traditional center door post. Fitted with the Jalpa engine and transmission, the Portofino was built by Italian coach builder Coggiola. As elegant inside as out, the Portofino boasted hand-sewn leather seats and a completely adjustable cockpit that allowed the seat, instru-

The first four-passenger, four-door, fully operational mid-engine "supercar" the world had seen, this 1987 Lamborghini Portofino marked the first use of Chrysler's cab-forward architecture, which was fine-tuned through a series of subsequent concept cars before becoming the Company's signature style.

The lineage of the Portofino can be seen in full-production cars such as these 1993 models, the Eagle Vision and the Dodge Intrepid.

ment panel and steering wheel to be repositioned to fit almost any driver.

In early 1988, Chrysler President Bob Lutz, General Operations Manager Tom Gale, Vehicle Engineering Chief François Castaing and Chrysler performance consultant Carroll Shelby (creator of the Shelby Cobra of the 1960s) held a series of meetings to establish guidelines for the creation of a high-performance sports car akin to the legendary Cobras. Only five months elapsed from the first meeting through the initial drawings at Chrysler's Highland Park Advanced Design Studio to final approval of a full-size clay model. On May 28, 1988, the Company began construction of the concept model for the auto show circuit: the two-seater sports car dubbed Viper. At its heart lay the engine, an all-aluminum version of the V-10 engine Chrysler was developing for the next generation of Dodge Ram pickups. Because no V-10s were yet available, Chrysler engineers grafted the front two cylinders of a 360 V-8 onto another 360 engine block. The Viper RT/10 prototype, painted Bright Viper Red, debuted on January 4, 1989, at the North American International Show in Detroit. The reviews were sensational, and the Viper moved from concept to production.

The Viper's big V-10 engine made the creation of a long hood and short rear deck necessary. Voluptuous and menacing, this concept car featured massive 17-in. tires mounted on unique three-spoke wheels, fiberglass bodywork, the now-classic front fender air extractors, side-mounted exhaust pipes, a wraparound sport bar and one item that failed to make it into the production model: a wraparound windshield with aerodynamically integrated side mirrors.

1988

■ Salman Rushdie publishes *The Satanic Verses,* for which the Ayatollah Khomeini imposes on him a *fatwa* ("death sentence") for blasphemy; the British government protests, and Rushdie goes into hiding.

1989

▲ Deng Xiaoping brutally suppresses the Prodemocracy Movement's student-led protests centered around Beijing's Tiananmen Square.

■ At the urging of U.S. President George Bush, Congress votes billions of dollars to bail out the corrupt and capsizing savings and loan industry.

▲ The Exxon *Valdez* causes the world's largest oil spill when it runs aground in Alaska.

■ The Berlin Wall separating Communist East Berlin from democratic West Berlin, long the emblem of the Cold War, is chipped away piece by piece by Germans determined to end the partition of their nation.

Digital Decade

HARDLY WERE THE 1990s underway before talk began of a new millennium. It may have had as much to do with the breadth of change taking place during the decade as with the annual countdown to the year 2000, since—as many popular historians pointed out—the 1990s might well be compared with the Industrial Revolution or the early Renaissance of the mid-1400s, when Gutenberg introduced movable type and transformed the printing of the written word. Long-established traditions and dearly held verities in politics, economics, science and social life fell by the wayside. Biotechnology put genetically engineered crops on the table, gene therapy promised a cure to previously incurable diseases, and the successful cloning of a sheep and the imminent mapping of the human genome raised issues about the very definition of life. Humble calculating machines called computers were transformed into personal tools of empowerment (a favorite 1990's word) by kids working in garages and rundown motels out West. The global computer grid known as the Internet broke free of its origins in the Defense Department ARPANET and the government science bureaucracy's NSFNet to become the "information superhighway," which incited a digital revolution, exploded established boundaries and changed the way people lived, worked, communicated and shopped. Such change hardly made optimism a keynote of the decade, and the anxieties and uncertainties it promoted were reflected in an inability to name the period at all. Instead, with the drone of new 24-hour news networks or the flash and zap of round-the-clock music videos playing constantly in the background, pundits talked of the post-modern world, post-Cold War politics, post-industrial society life.

In truth, there may not have been that much to be optimistic about in the early years of the decade. America's finances were in trouble again after years of military buildup and heavy deficit spending had caused a recession and forced President George Bush to renege on a famous promise he made when he asked Americans watching him on television to read his lips as he delivered his clearest campaign statement: "No new taxes." The reversal cost him the reelection he thought ensured by his handling of that first post-modern, post-Cold War conflict, the Gulf War. Watching the glitzy, digitalized combat on CNN, most Americans approved of the new war with its preprogrammed smart bombs atop Tomahawk cruise missiles sweeping down chimneys and slipping through the air shafts of bunkers, and not least because the United States managed to kill some 200,000 Iraqis while losing only 148 of its own. But Bush's 91 percent approval rating—the highest ever for a president—in the immediate post-Persian Gulf period collapsed in the face of the nation's economic backsliding. As corporate America experienced a series of mergers, acquisitions and restructurings, large companies laid off employees by the tens of thousands. In 1991 alone, American firms cut more than 2,400 jobs on average every business day. Detroit's Big Three—Chrysler, Ford and General Motors—posted losses of nearly $7.5 billion. Where employees had been making salaries that outpaced inflation, they now fretted over slashed payrolls and shrinking benefits—that is, if they managed to keep their jobs. Not only had President Bush taxed them, he had failed to protect them. As the 1992 elections rolled around, Bush was presiding over a $4 trillion national debt and an eight-year high in unemployment. Just enough Republican and independent malcontents, once solid Reagan people, voted for the quirky third party candidate Ross Perot to put the first baby boomer in the White House—William Jefferson Clinton.

The decade opened with the Gulf War, the first fully televised foreign war.

Chrysler meanwhile was working to reverse the decline that a mid-1980s buying binge, an aging product line and the recent recession had created. A new generation of managers, engineers and designers proceeded to dazzle everyone with an unprecedented string of design and market successes. Exciting concept cars engendered equally exciting products, from specialty image cars such as the Dodge Viper and Plymouth Prowler to luxury sport-utility vehicles from Jeep and Dodge to aggressively styled pickups and the cab-forward LH passenger car line. Quality soared under the new platform team approach, and Chrysler's mid-sized cars began winning design awards even as the Company broke into a market segment long thought inaccessible to American automakers with its new small car, the Neon. Both the redesigned minivan and the restyled LH and LHS models set the new design standard for the industry. The minivan was named "Car of the Year," despite the fact that it was not exactly a car, and later in the decade so was the resurrected Chrysler 300, created to be marketable in Europe but also enjoying tremendous domestic sales. Gone were the morale and quality problems of recent decades as the Company settled comfortably into its new headquarters in Auburn Hills, Michigan.

Under Bill Clinton, Americans too were enjoying a return to prosperity. Partly, the good times had to do with Clinton's reinvention of the Democratic party as a fiscally responsible steward determined to eliminate the deficits of the Reagan years, but they probably owed more to the incredible boom in the communications industry. In 1991, Tim Berners-Lee had invented a sort of electronic filing cabinet in which personal computer users could connect to other computers and retrieve documents by typing in key words. By

1993, college programmers produced search engines for this World Wide Web, which transformed the Internet from a computer network into a global marketplace. By the time White House scandals led to the first Republican majority in both the House and Senate in 40 years, Americans turned to Web sites as well as cable television for the latest news of Clinton's misdeeds, an outbreak of ebola in Africa or yet another trial of the century. Even while political wrangling in Washington brought the government to virtual gridlock, initial offerings by "dot com" enterprises set off a bull market on Wall Street the likes of which the country had never seen. Traditional companies scampered to establish outposts on the Web, consumer purchasing on the Internet soared into the billions and business-to-business e-commerce into the hundreds of billions.

As the world went digital, Europeans groused about the Americanization of the entire planet. And certainly, there were a lot of Americans on the Web. Some 80 million of them owned personal computers by the late 1990s. The stock market of the 1980s, bullish on mergers, acquisitions and junk bonds, had belonged to the select few, but the market explosion of the mid- to late 1990s belonged—almost—to everyone. Half the families in America traded stocks in what had become the greatest democratization of Wall Street since the 1920s. Corporate America dressed down, and not just on Fridays, as ever younger entrepreneurs made fortunes in the chairs of the hottest companies listed on the high-tech dominated NASDAQ exchange. Eighties-style prosperity and big spending returned,

and more people bought homes that, like the SUVs parked in their driveways, grew bigger each year. Though Federal Reserve Board Chairman Alan Greenspan, the public's Mahareshi of finance, strove mightily to keep prosperity on track, it was increasingly evident that some day something would have to give. In an economic system that was now truly global, Chrysler executives were concerned about the "Perfect Storm" facing the always volatile auto industry, especially for a company with little presence outside North America. They opened negotiations with another group of auto executives they had first talked to when trying to prevent a hostile takeover a few years earlier. In 1998—to ensure their future in an ever more competitive industry—Chrysler and Daimler-Benz, the world leader in automotive technology and quality, merged to form DaimlerChrysler.

The baby boomers take charge.

■ After the collapse of Communist Yugoslavia, ethnic war breaks out in the Balkans.

■ The U.S. Fish and Wildlife Service adds the northern spotted owl to the endangered species list, sparking confrontation between environmentalists and loggers in the Pacific Northwest.

1991

■ When a military coup fails to depose Russian President Mikhail Gorbachev, the Communist party is outlawed and the Soviet Union falls apart.

Design Moves Forward

Thomas Gale became vice president of Product Design at Chrysler in 1985. Joining the Company in 1967, he had worked his way up through the ranks, and his ascension marked a new era in Chrysler product design. Like Virgil Exner before him, Gale fought against the restraints on design; in his case it was reliance on the K platform. K-Cars could be stretched or gussied up, but the Company resisted changing the fundamentals as insurmountably expensive. Like Exner, Gale used concept cars to confront conventional wisdom and explore different styles, ultimately producing a look that dominated Chrysler products in the 1990s—the "cab-forward" design.

To the delight of auto show patrons and the automotive press, Chrysler began in 1987 to field a series of award-winning concept cars such as the Portofino, Atlantic Citadel, Viper, Optima, Voyager III, Neon, Cirrus, 300, Epic, Ecco and Prowler. Most of Gale's concept cars, like Exner's, were fully operational, but unlike Exner, Gale was part of a Company management group determined to shake things up. The old Chrysler team toyed with putting Exner's 1955 Falcon roadster into production but rejected the idea. By contrast, the

In addition to running Product Design, Thomas Gale, by the early 1990s, headed Chrysler's International Operations. From 1991 until June 1993, he served as general manager of Minivan Operations, which meant he was in charge of the "platform team" developing the Company's crown jewels, the next generation of minivans. When Gale announced his retirement in 2000, he served as executive vice president of Chrysler Product Development and Design and general manager of Passenger Car Operations. His ascendancy marked the coming of age of design as a fully integrated function in the Corporation and put Chrysler in the front ranks of innovative automotive styling.

Proud of his affection for the "hot-rods" of his youth, Gale designed the Prowler in homage. Much like the radically sporty Viper, the Prowler was a high-profile signal that at Chrysler design was certainly no longer stodgy and not merely serviceable. Design was also an aesthetic statement, one that could be playful as well as functional.

new Chrysler team took the new Viper and—backed by Gale, hard-driving Chrysler President Bob Lutz and Vehicle Engineering Chief François Castaing—pushed it from concept to production in just three years.

When the revitalized Company management called for a bold new line of passenger cars for the 1993 model year, Gale was poised to create the popular LH cars. Based on the Portofino concept, their cab-forward design maximized interior volume and passenger room by drawing the imaginary center line of the steeply angled windshield toward the center of the front wheels and pushing the back wheels rearward relative to the

bumper. Low in front, high in back, with belt lines rising sharply and roofs no longer parallel to the ground, the LHs caught the eye of both consumers and the automobile industry. By 1993, Gale—a designer (though trained as an engineer) in a company traditionally dominated by engineers—was a member of Chrysler's upper management. His lieutenants on the 350-person Product Design staff, Trevor Creed, Neil Walling and John Herlitz, were ensconced at the new Chrysler Technology Center in Auburn Hills and having an enormous impact on car design as, once again, Chrysler reshaped automobile architecture.

In 1993, the cab-forward LH cars Chrysler Concorde, Dodge Intrepid and Eagle Vision received the Industrial Designers Society of America Gold Industrial Design Excellence Award (IDEA) for transportation as "landmark" vehicles that "reset the bar much higher for competitors." Cab-forward design would continue to characterize the second generation of LH cars, whose striking looks were forecast by the 1996 LHS concept car shown here.

The new design itself became a subject for Chrysler advertising.

As you can see, we haven't merely altered the Chrysler stereotype. We've annihilated it. The lumbering luxoboat is gone. In its place is the Concorde. It's got more horsepower than cars with much higher price tags ... namely, the BMW 525i, the Infiniti J30t, and even the Lexus ES 300. Then, on a slalom course, the Concorde outmaneuvered a Nissan Maxima, an Audi Quattro V-8, and an Infiniti Q45. A feat made possible, in part, by the

It overpowered the Infiniti J30t, outmaneuvered the Nissan Maxima and totally destroyed the Chrysler stereotype.

Concorde's "cab-forward" architecture, which gives the car a wide track for precise handling. Not to mention a cavernous interior. Leaving you plenty of room to enjoy such luxury appointments as an available moon roof, CD player and leather-trimmed seats. Safety features like driver and front passenger air bags and four-wheel disc anti-lock brakes come standard. We think a drive in the Concorde will change your opinion about American luxury cars. It might even change your car. For more information, call 1-800-4A-CHRYSLER.

CHRYSLER

"Leadership in this business does not always mean listening to the consumer. It is a company's responsibility to present possibilities, to anticipate what the customer might like if it were offered."

—BOB LUTZ

▲ The Chrysler Technology Center (CTC) is dedicated.

■ William Smith, nephew of Senator Edward Kennedy, is tried and found not guilty on charges of raping a woman at the Kennedy estate in Palm Beach.

■ During Senate confirmation hearings, University of Oklahoma law professor Anita Hill charges Supreme Court nominee Clarence Thomas with sexual harassment when they were colleagues in the 1980s.

■ Los Angeles Lakers star Earvin "Magic" Johnson announces he has the HIV virus that causes AIDS and retires from basketball.

■ British scientist Tim Berners-Lee invents the World Wide Web, a computer Internet network used to exchange information and messages.

▲ Democrat Bill Clinton defeats Republican incumbent George Bush and becomes the first baby boomer to hold the office of president.

■ Chicago's Carol Mosley Braun becomes the first black woman elected to serve in the U.S. Senate.

▲ A U.S.-led, UN-sanctioned military intervention occurs in Somalia where famine has killed 300,000 and tribal conflict has led to social anarchy.

■ The United States and Russia sign an agreement officially ending the Cold War.

Platform Teams and a New Regime

Conservative design, a perception of product quality problems, a corporate buying spree and an economic downturn once again brought Chrysler Corporation to the edge of disaster by the early 1990s. Yet the Corporation was to undergo a remarkable turnaround, only this time instead of federal loan guarantees there would be new plants, new products and the new attitudes of a new regime with a vision of where to take the Company and how.

A decade earlier, the 1979 Loan Guarantee Act had mandated that Chrysler and the United Auto Workers act together on a program to improve quality. In 1984, a group of young employees called the Youth Advocacy Council, following an intensive study of Honda Motors, sought to change the system by suggesting that management create cross-functional teams to produce cars. In 1987, Chrysler's acquisition of American Motors brought with it a major champion of the team concept, former Renault engineer François Castaing. Along with head designer Tom Gale, Chrysler President Bob Lutz and others, Castaing put together Chrysler's first cross-functional team to work on the LH family of cars. In

The Neon, a "happy faced," bug-eyed, cab-forward subcompact concept car that debuted at the Detroit Auto Show in January 1991, was created to appeal in looks and price to a young audience.

The rapid development of the Viper from concept to production was something of a test run for the platform team concept. Here "Team Viper" gathers around the product, which became an early icon of the new direction at Chrysler.

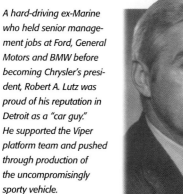

A hard-driving ex-Marine who held senior management jobs at Ford, General Motors and BMW before becoming Chrysler's president, Robert A. Lutz was proud of his reputation in Detroit as a "car guy." He supported the Viper platform team and pushed through production of the uncompromisingly sporty vehicle.

At the 1996 Indianapolis 500, Chrysler President Bob Lutz drove the pace car, a Viper GTS. Above is a Viper GTR from the Museum's collection.

1989 and 1990, the team moved from Chrysler headquarters in Highland Park to the Liberty "Skunkworks" in Auburn Hills to distance itself physically as well as symbolically from the way cars were traditionally developed. By the time Robert Eaton, who was president of General Motors of Europe, came on board in 1992 to replace the retiring Lee Iacocca as chairman and chief executive officer, Chrysler Corporation had restructured around the platform team concept. Housed in the new Chrysler Technology Center, whose very design encouraged cross-functional teamwork, representatives from various departments now worked together on a single vehicle from development through production.

Chrysler used facets of the platform team concept to develop the Viper, and cross-functional teams played a role in the development of the Jeep Cherokee in the early 1990s, but proof of the theory came in late 1992 with the introduction of the LH cars, which enjoyed sell-out success. Quick on their heels, the revamped minivan (named *Motor Trend*'s "Car of the Year" in 1995), Jeep Grand Cherokee and Dodge Ram pickup, plus the new subcompact Neon, underscored the success of platform teams. Today there are five such teams at Chrysler—Small Car, Minivan, Large Car, Jeep and Truck.

The totally redesigned 1994 Dodge Ram reestablished Chrysler Corporation as a contender in the full-size pickup market and helped confirm the Company's market leadership in design.

Replacing Lee Iacocca as Chrysler Corporation's chairman and CEO, Robert Eaton presided over the Company's renascence in the 1990s and played a key role in its merger with Germany's Daimler-Benz at the end of the decade.

Chrysler Corporation's 15-story office tower, with its all-glass exterior, open atriums and flexible office space, was designed to foster teamwork, communication and creativity.

The Chrysler CTC Complex.

1993

- A van loaded with explosives and planted by Muslim fundamentalists explodes in the parking garage under New York's World Trade Center, killing 6 and injuring more than 1,000.

- Folks everywhere begin to "surf the Web" after University of Illinois programmers release Mosaic, the first software to put the World Wide Web within reach of virtually every computer.

- Israeli Prime Minister Yitzhak Rabin and Arab leader Yassir Arafat shake hands on the White House lawn after signing a peace accord between Israel and the Palestine Liberation Organization (PLO).

- *Jurassic Park,* directed by Steven Spielberg, becomes the highest grossing movie of all time.

- Writer Toni Morrison becomes the first African American to win the Nobel Prize in literature.

1993

- Congress passes the Brady Bill, named for former President Ronald Reagan's press secretary James Brady, requiring a waiting period of five days for the purchase of handguns.

- Chicago Bulls superstar Michael Jordan, grieving the loss of his father and beset by questions about his gambling, announces he will retire from basketball.

- President Bill Clinton signs into law the North American Free Trade Agreement (NAFTA), which will phase out all tariffs and trade barriers among the U.S., Canada and Mexico over 14 years.

- Daimler-Benz begins to assemble its first cars in Mexico.

1994

- After spending a lifetime in jail, Nelson Mandela becomes the first black president of South Africa.

- The first Chrysler LHS models and the Dodge Neon debut.

- David Filo and Jerry Yang launch a Web search engine called Yahoo!, which they developed as graduate students at Stanford.

American (and European) Dreams

Two of Chrysler's most admired concept cars are the Atlantic Coupe and the Chronos. Inspired by the legendary Bugatti Atlantique of the 1930s, the Atlantic Coupe debuted in 1995. Although its pontoon fenders and flowing lines harkened back to an earlier age of elegant international automobile design, the Atlantic featured thoroughly modern all-steel unitized construction, four-wheel independent suspension, four-wheel power disc brakes and the same AutoStick transmission available on DaimlerChrysler's current cars.

In 1997, the Chrysler design staff introduced the Chrysler Chronos. Like the Atlantic, it was an example of "heritage design," clearly inspired by the much-trumpeted 1953 Chrysler d'Elegance. Long-hooded, with a short rear deck like the Atlantic, the Chronos featured a hand-formed steel body, a hand-wrapped leather steering wheel and hand-sewn leather seating. The 4,200-lb. Chronos, which cost $2 million to develop, was built on a Chrysler Concorde platform and came equipped with a four-wheel independent suspension derived from the Dodge Viper. Both the Chronos and the Atlantic are fully operational vehicles, called in the automobile world "runners," as well as dream cars.

This 1995 Chrysler Atlantic Coupe continues its "heritage design" on the inside, with leather-trimmed seating for four and classic gold-trimmed watch-face gauges. Under the hood, its "retro" engine, a 4.0-liter inline eight-cylinder with dual overhead cams and 32 valves, employs modern design technology to produce 325 hp.

Unlike the 1953 Chrysler d'Elegance whose design it echoes, this 1997 Chrysler Chronos has under its long hood a 6.0-liter, 350 hp, overhead cam V-10 engine.

1994

■ An early morning earthquake registering 6.7 on the Richter scale rocks Los Angeles, collapsing buildings and freeways and killing 61.

■ Paula Jones, a former Arkansas state employee, seeking $700,000 and a public apology, files suit against President Bill Clinton for sexual harassment.

■ Daimler-Benz begins a factory in Tuscaloosa, Alabama.

■ O.J. Simpson is arrested for the murders of his ex-wife Nicole Brown Simpson and her friend Ronald Goldman.

1995

▼ For the first time in 40 years, the Republican party takes control of both the House and Senate.

The Walter P. Chrysler Museum

From an assemblage of vintage autos displayed at Chrysler's old Highland Park headquarters or stored in remote corners of Company property, the Walter P. Chrysler Museum developed into an exquisitely designed and professionally run facility in just a few short years. After Chrysler Corporation moved to the Auburn Hills complex, a group of executives decided to gather these collections together in a single museum building. A board of directors for the Museum, originally including Tom Gale, François Castaing, John Herlitz, Frank Fountain, Kathy Oswald, Steve Harris and A. C. "Bud" Liebler, decided to create, in Liebler's words, "a place where people could learn how important...cars were in their own day and in creating the society we live in today."

The collection at first was not representative of the entire scope of the Company's history. Product Planner Ken Mack began searching for automobiles to fill the gaps. Octie Hamm of the Vehicle Engineering Operations, along with retired engineers Bruce Thomas, Bill Ridenour and Mike Krag, investigated cars, searched for parts and supervised the actual

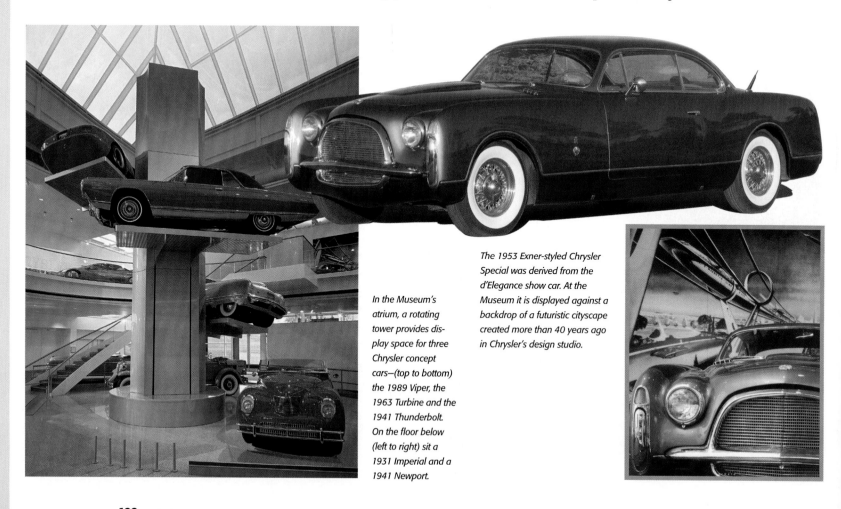

In the Museum's atrium, a rotating tower provides display space for three Chrysler concept cars—(top to bottom) the 1989 Viper, the 1963 Turbine and the 1941 Thunderbolt. On the floor below (left to right) sit a 1931 Imperial and a 1941 Newport.

The 1953 Exner-styled Chrysler Special was derived from the d'Elegance show car. At the Museum it is displayed against a backdrop of a futuristic cityscape created more than 40 years ago in Chrysler's design studio.

restoration work. All this behind the scenes collecting and restoring began even before ground was broken for the new building designed by architects Giffels and Associates.

Operating the museum as a public facility was entrusted to Corporate Communications with Rita McKay named Museum director. The Company hired Design Craftsmen of Midland, Michigan, to design and build the exhibits. As exhibit development and building construction were underway, Barry Dressel, former head of the Detroit Historical Museums, came on board as Museum manager and was part of a team that fine-tuned and oversaw the execution of the plan.

The Museum opened on October 5, 1999. With nearly 60,000 square feet of space, the granite and glass building includes exhibit areas, a theatre, catering facilities, offices and a gift shop. Special features include a rotating tower of concept cars tilted at a slight angle for easy viewing in the atrium, short films, a corporate "family tree," dioramas and computer interactive "time stations." Throughout the Museum, visitors may stop at interactive exhibit stations where, for example, they may turn a steering wheel to experience "finger-tip" power steering or push a brake pedal

A life-size figure of Walter P. Chrysler, cast from his great-grandson Frank Rhodes, works in his workshop.

The 1934 DeSoto Airflow once owned by Carl Breer is a prized vehicle in the Museum's collection.

Chrysler's role in the American war effort during World War II is told in a diorama featuring two GIs and their 1943 Jeep MB.

■ As Chrysler's new head-quarters opens officially in Auburn Hills, the Company introduces a redesigned minivan, the Prowler and the Sebring convertible.

■ Suspected of being the terrorist dubbed by the press the "Unabomber," Ted Kaczynski is arrested by the FBI in Lincoln, Montana.

■ The Hale-Bopp comet appears in the earth's night sky for the first time in 4,200 years.

■ Researchers at the Roslin Institute in Edinburgh, Scotland, create a sheep named Dolly from the cells of an adult sheep, making her the world's first cloned mammal.

■ Twenty-one-year-old Tiger
Woods becomes the first
African American, and
the youngest man, to win
the Masters championship
in golf.

■ In its initial public stock
offering Amazon.com,
which began as an on-line
bookstore but grew to
hawk everything from
electronics to lawn chairs,
makes its founder Jeff
Bezo a billionaire though
the company has yet to
turn a profit.

■ Daimler-Benz debuts its
U.S.-built M class cars and
purchases the Ford Heavy
Diesel Truck Operations,
which it renames Sterling.

■ Timothy McVeigh, an army
veteran with ties to right-
wing militia groups, is convicted and sentenced to
death for the 1995 bomb-
ing of the Federal Building
in Oklahoma City.

▲ NASA's spacecraft
Pathfinder lands on Mars
and deploys a small roving
vehicle called *Sojourner*.

to demonstrate the difference between mechanical and hydraulic brakes.

Two dioramas are devoted to Walter P. Chrysler. In one, Chrysler works in his workshop; nearby sits his famous toolbox. In the other, Chrysler meets in his office with the Three Musketeers—Fred Zeder, Owen Skelton and Carl Breer—all portrayed in life-size re-creations. In another diorama upstairs, a 1970 Dodge Challenger T/A "cruises" past a recreation of Woodward Avenue's legendary Totem Pole drive-in restaurant in

suburban Detroit. Other vignettes show Dad bringing home a new 1956 Dodge D500 and World War II GIs reading a map next to their 1943 Jeep MB.

On the lower level of the Museum, "Boss Chrysler's Garage" includes a simulated race track with the Dodge 330 Super Stock "Color Me Gone" car, a 1953 Hudson Hornet, a 1969 Dodge Charger Daytona and a 1978 Dodge Li'l Red Express.

The Museum still actively collects automobiles to add to its collection. The current collection includes

This 1937 Dodge 1/2-ton panel truck featured a "hump-back" or double-level roof, first intro-duced in 1933 and continued in production until 1938.

On the upper level, the Museum displays a cross-section of Chrysler's his-tory. Here, the turbulent 1980s are represented by the K-Car platform vehi-cles (center), flanked by a 1957 Imperial (foreground), a 1975 Cordoba (left), a 1993 Jeep Grand Cherokee (center background) and on the top of the tower display the 1989 Dodge Viper concept car (right background).

more than 200 vehicles and is still growing. The Museum displays more than 60 vehicles ranging from the 1961 Metropolitan, a diminutive bath-tub of a car weighing in at 1,890 lb. to the 5,070-lb. 1941 4 x 4 Dodge Army command car, from the 1902 Rambler Model C runabout that puttered along at a cruising speed of 14 mph with 4 hp to the 1965 A/FX drag car that pulled a whopping 600+ hp from its 426 cu. in. Hemi V-8 engine.

In addition to collecting, displaying and caring for the collections, the Museum publishes a quarterly magazine, *Forward,* for members.

The first on-site museum built by an active North American automotive company, the Museum celebrates the millions of cars and trucks built by Chrysler and the companies it grew from, merged with or purchased. It also tells the important story of the thousands of people involved in the creation of these vehicles— from Walter P. Chrysler himself to line workers, race car drivers, dealers and advertising pitch men.

In "Boss Chrysler's Garage," the publicly accessible storage area on the Museum's lower level, a simulated race track features Chrysler's performance cars from the 1950s, 1960s and 1970s.

This 1957 Dodge ½-ton sweptside pickup is among the Museum's collection of Dodge trucks. This model was introduced to compete with the Ford Ranchero and the Chevrolet El Camino.

1998

■ In Jonesboro, Arkansas, two boys, ages 11 and 13, kill four schoolgirls and one teacher outside their middle school during a false fire alarm–the first in string of such shootings in American public schools.

▲ Based on independent prosecutor Kenneth Starr's report to Congress, the House votes to impeach President Bill Clinton on a number of counts, including perjury during the Paula Jones case.

▲ Baseball players Mark McGwire and Sammy Sousa break Roger Maris's 1961 record of home runs in a single season when they knock, respectively, 70 and 66 balls out of the park.

■ Former professional wrestler Jesse "the Body" Ventura is elected as an independent to be governor of Minnesota.

■ Chrysler merges with Daimler-Benz to create DaimlerChrysler.

1924 CHRYSLER B-70 PHAETON

The Museum Collection

This listing consists of vehicles generally on view in the Museum in 1999 and 2000, not including those shown in special exhibitions. Reserve and display fleet collection vehicles are not included.

Chrysler

1924 Model 70 Four-Door Phaeton *Photo on page 35*

This car, designed by the famed engineers Zeder, Skelton and Breer, was something new to the automobile market, a high-compression, high-speed six-cylinder L-head engine that developed 68 hp. This prototype had two-wheel mechanical brakes. Production models had four-wheel hydraulic brakes.

Length: 170 in. (432 cm)
Wheelbase: 112 in. (286 cm)
Weight: 2,785 lb. (1,263 kg)
Engine: Inline L-head six-cylinder
Transmission: Three-speed manual
Displacement: 201 cu. in. (3,294 cu cm)
Horsepower: 68
Cruising speed: 60 mph (100 km/h)
Price: $1,395

1931 Imperial CG Dual Cowl Phaeton *Photo on page 43*

An officially recognized Full Classic®, this car is one of the most beautiful vehicles ever produced by Chrysler. This was the first year of an eight-cylinder engine that set 12 Class B stock car records.

Length: 213 in. (541 cm)
Wheelbase: 145 in. (368 cm)
Weight: 4,645 lb. (2107 kg)
Engine: Inline eight-cylinder
Transmission: Selective sliding gear four-speed
Displacement: 385 cu. in. (6311 cu cm)
Cruising speed: 65 mph (100+ km/h)
Price: $3,575

1934 Airflow CU Sedan *Photo on page 51*

Hailed as the first modern automobile, the Airflow was influential world-wide. Despite its many advances, it was never a success in the United States. (Donor: George Evory.)

Length: 207.5 in. (527 cm)
Wheelbase: 122.8 in. (315 cm)
Weight: 3,760 lb. (1,706 kg)
Engine: Inline eight-cylinder
Transmission: Three-speed manual with automatic overdrive
Displacement: 298 cu. in. (4,496 cu cm)

Horsepower: 122
Cruising speed: 65 mph (100+ km/h)
Price: $1,345

1936 Chrysler Imperial Airflow C-10

The Chrysler Imperial Sedan was the most popular of the Airflows in 1936. For the first time they featured an all-steel roof. (Donated to the museum by Hardy Trolander, 2000.)

Length: 216 in. (549 cm)
Wheelbase: 128 in. (325 cm)
Weight: 4,175 lbs. (1,894 kg)
Engine: Inline L-head eight-cylinder
Transmission: Three-speed manual with automatic overdrive
Displacement: 323.5 cu. in. (5,301 cu cm)
Horse power: 130
Cruising speed: 65 mph (100+ km/h)
Price: $1,475

1940 Newport Dual Cowl Phaeton *Photo on page 61*

This special phaeton was designed by Ralph Roberts and built by Brigg's LeBaron division. One of the six constructed served as the pace car for the 1941 Indianapolis 500. The other five were used at auto shows and in dealer showroom displays throughout the country.

Length: 228 in. (585 cm)
Wheelbase: 145.5 in. (373 cm)
Weight: N.A.

Engine: Inline eight-cylinder
Transmission: Three-speed semiautomatic
Displacement: 323 cu. in. (5,295 cu cm)
Horsepower: 143
Cruising speed: 60 mph (100 km/h)
Price: N.A.

1941 Thunderbolt Two-Passenger Coupe *Photo on page 60*

This two-passenger retractable hardtop coupe, designed by Alex Tremulis and built by LeBaron, featured an automatic, one-piece metal top that disappeared into a compartment behind the cockpit. Concealed headlamps, side windows and deck lid were all electrically controlled. Six Thunderbolts were built for display across the country.

Length: 205 in. (521 cm)
Wheelbase: 127.5 in. (324 cm)
Weight: N.A.
Engine: Inline eight-cylinder
Transmission: Three-speed semiautomatic
Displacement: 323.5 cu. in. (5,303 cu cm)
Horsepower: 137
Cruising speed: 60 mph (100 km/h)
Price: N.A.

1948 Town & Country Convertible Coupe *Photo on page 69*

The Town & Country, first introduced as a station wagon before World War II, was available as a convertible and sedan.

Length: 227.75 in. (578.4 cm)
Wheelbase: 127 in. (324 cm)
Weight: 4,332 lb. (1,965 kg)
Engine: Inline L-head eight-cylinder
Transmission: Three-speed manual with Fluid Drive
Displacement: 323.5 cu. in (3,294 cu cm)
Horsepower: 135
Cruising speed: 65 mph (100+ km/h)
Price: $3,420

1951 New Yorker Convertible *Photo on page 79*

This convertible's new FirePower engine, called the "Hemi," had a hemispherical combustion chamber based on research begun in the 1930s. It was the most powerful of the postwar overhead valve engines developed by the Big Three.

Length: 213.75 in. (543 cm)
Wheelbase: 131.5 in. (334 cm)
Weight: 4,460 lb. (2,023 kg)
Engine: Hemi-head V-8 with overhead valves and dual rocker shafts
Transmission: Two-speed dual-range semiautomatic
Displacement: 331.1 cu. in. (5,427 cu cm)
Horsepower: 180
Cruising speed: 70+ mph (113+ km/h)
Price: $3,941

1953 Chrysler Special *Photo on page 128*

Designed by Chrysler and built by Italian coach builder Carrozzeria Ghia, the Italian-fabricated car body was placed on a Chrysler chassis.

Length: 204.5 in. (518 cm)
Wheelbase: 125 in. (318 cm)
Weight: 3,600 lb. (1,633 kg)
Engine: Hemi-head V-8
Transmission: Fluid-Torque
Displacement: 331 cu. in. (5,427 cu cm)
Horsepower: 180
Cruising speed: 70 mph (113 km/h)
Price: N.A.

1955 300 Sport Coupe *Photo on page 80*

Performance and styling combined to make the 300 popular with consumers and race enthusiasts alike.

Length: 218.6 in. (358 cm)
Wheelbase: 126 in. (320 cm)
Weight: 4,005 lb. (1,817 kg)
Engine: Hemi-head V-8 with two four-barrel carburetors, performance cam with solid lifters and dual exhausts
Transmission: Two-speed PowerFlite
Displacement: 331.1 cu. in. (5,427 cu cm)
Horsepower: 300
Cruising speed: 70+ mph (113 km/h)
Price: $4,109

1957 300 C Sport Coupe *Photo on page 83*

Capable of 145 mph and 0 to 60 in 7.7 seconds, this was one of stylist Virgil Exner's most successful "fin cars."

Length: 219.2 (557 cm)
Wheelbase: 126 in. (320 cm)
Weight: 4,235 lb. (1,921 kg)
Engine: Hemi-head V-8 with two four-barrel carburetors
Transmission: Three-speed Torqueflite automatic
Displacement: 392 cu. in. (6,475 cu cm)
Horsepower: 375
Cruising speed: 70+ mph (113 km/h)
Price: $4,929

1957 Imperial Southhampton Hardtop *Photo on page 82*

Considered one of Virgil Exner's finest designs, the Imperial featured curved side window glass, an industry first, along with a compound curved windshield.

Length: 224 in. (569 cm)
Wheelbase: 129 in. (328 cm)
Weight: 4,920 lb. (2,232 kg)
Engine: Hemi-head V-8 with overhead values
Transmission: Push-button three-speed Torqueflite automatic
Displacement: 392 cu. in. (6,425 cu cm)
Horsepower: 325
Cruising speed: 70+ mph (112 km/h)
Price: $5,406

1961 300 G Sport Coupe

This car represents the second year for ram induction on the 300 and the last year for fin designs.

Length: 219.9 in. (558 cm)
Wheelbase: 126 in. (320 cm)
Weight: 4,260 lb. (1,932 kg)
Engine: V-8
Transmission: Push-button three-speed automatic
Displacement: 413 cu. in. (6,769 cu cm)
Horsepower: 375
Cruising speed: 70+ mph (113 km/h)
Price: $5,441

1963 Turbine Two-Door Sport Coupe   *Photo on page 89*

This is one of 50 identical vehicles that housed the experimental regenerative turbine engine. The body was designed by Chrysler and built by Ghia of Turan, Italy, at a rate of one per week from October 1963 to October 1964.

Length: 204 in. (518 cm)
Wheelbase: 110 in. (279 cm)
Weight: N.A.
Engine: Turbine
Transmission: Three-speed automatic
Displacement: N.A.
Horsepower: 130
Cruising speed: 70+ mph (113 km/h)
Price: N.A.

1970 300-H Sport Coupe   *Photo on page 90*

A special high-performance limited-edition Chrysler modified by Hurst Performance Production Corporation. Only 501 were built.

Length: 224.7 in. (571 cm)
Wheelbase: 124 in. (315 cm)
Weight: 4,135 lb. (1,876 kg)
Engine: V-8
Transmission: Three-speed Torqueflite automatic
Displacement: 440 cu. in. (7,212 cu cm)
Horsepower: 375
Cruising speed: 70+ mph (113 km/h)
Price: $5,842

1976 Cordoba Hardtop Coupe   *Photo on page 101*

The Cordoba garnered 60 percent of the 1975 Chrysler sales. The "new, small Chrysler" reversed a long-standing Chrysler refusal to sell "junior editions."

Length: 215.3 in. (547 cm)
Wheelbase: 115 in. (291 cm)
Weight: 4,035 lb. (1,830 kg)

Engine: V-8
Transmission: Three-speed Torqueflite automatic
Displacement: 360 cu. in. (5,904 cu cm)
Horsepower: 170
Cruising speed: 70+ mph (113 km/h)
Price: $5,581

1986 LeBaron Town & Country Convertible   *Photo on page 105*

Introduced in 1982, these were the first U.S.-built convertibles in several years.

Length: 179.2 in. (455 cm)
Wheelbase: 100.3 in. (255 cm)
Weight: 2,800 lb. (1,270 kg)
Engine: Inline overhead cam four-cylinder turbocharged
Transmission: Three-speed automatic
Displacement: 135 cu. in. (2,212 cu cm)
Horsepower: 146
Cruising speed: 70+ mph (113 km/h)
Price: $17,595

1987 LeBaron Convertible

This specially modified convertible paced the Indianapolis 500. It was modified to do 150 mph.

Length: 184.9 in. (470 cm)
Wheelbase: 100.3 in. (255 cm)
Weight: 2,786 lb. (1,264 kg)
Engine: Inline four-cylinder
Transmission: Five-speed manual
Displacement: 153 cu. in. (2,508 cu cm)
Horsepower: 230
Cruising speed: 70+ mph (113 km/h)
Price: N.A.

1987 Portofino Concept   *Photo on page 116*

Forerunner of "cab forward" design.

Length: 180 in. (457 cm)
Wheelbase: 122 in. (310 cm)
Weight: N.A.
Engine: V-8
Transmission: Five-speed manual
Displacement: 212 cu. in. (3,294 cu cm)
Horsepower: 225
Cruising speed: 70+ mph (113 km/h)
Price: N.A.

1992 LeBaron Modified Coupe

Bruce Hertel set several world records in production class, including a 196-mph flying mile in this car. All components came from MOPAR.

Length: 180 in. (457 cm)
Wheelbase: 100.3 in. (254.5 cm)
Weight: 2,960 lb. (1,343 kg)
Engine: Inline overhead cam four-cylinder turbocharged
Transmission: Five-speed manual
Displacement: 120 cu. in. (2,000 cu cm)
Horsepower: 410

1994 Atlantic Four-Passenger Coupe   *Photo on page 126*

The Atlantic, which made its debut in 1995, draws its graceful lines and stunning beauty from the late 1930s, an era of automotive design unsurpassed in style and elegance.

Length: 200 in. (508 cm)
Wheelbase: 124.5 in. (316 cm)
Weight: N.A.
Engine: Inline eight-cylinder
Transmission: Five-speed manual
Displacement: 244 cu. in. (4,000 cu cm)
Horsepower: 325
Cruising speed: 80+ mph (129 km/h)
Price: N.A.

DeSoto

1929 Series K Roadster   *Photo on page 38*

More than 500 dealers signed up to sell the new DeSoto, sight-unseen, when it was announced in the *Detroit Free Press* on May 6, 1928. The DeSoto provided comfort and style for a moderate price.

Length: 192 in. (488 cm)
Wheelbase: 109.75 in. (279 cm)
Weight: 2,350 lb. (1,066 kg)
Engine: Inline six-cylinder
Transmission: Three-speed manual
Displacement: 174.9 cu. in. (2,867 cu cm)

Horsepower: 55
Cruising speed: 50 mph (81 km/h)
Price: $845

1934 DeSoto Airflow Series SE   *Photo on page 129*

The DeSoto Airflow model developed directly from the Trifon Special concept car, and in 1934, every DeSoto produced was an Airflow. That year, the DeSoto Airflow set 32 stock car racing records.

Length: 196 in. (503 cm)
Wheelbase: 115.5 in. (293 cm.)
Weight: 3,378 lbs. (1,533 kg.)
Engine: Inline L-head six-cylinder
Transmission: Three-speed manual with Freewheeling
Displacement: 241.5 cu. in. (3,957 cu cm)
Horse power: 100
Cruising speed: 65 mph (100 + km/h)
Price: $995

Dodge

1915 Model 30-35 Four-Door Touring   *Photo on page 25*

After producing the engines and other components for Ford and others for over ten years, the Dodges began producing their own vehicle in late 1914. The tough vehicle they produced added "dependability" to the dictionary.

Length: 192 in. (488 cm)
Wheelbase: 110 in. (279 cm)
Weight: 2,220 lb. (998 kg)
Engine: Inline L-head four-cylinder
Transmission: Three-speed manual
Displacement: 212 cu. in. (3,496 cu cm)
Horsepower: 35
Cruising speed: 35 mph (56 km/h)
Price: $785

1939 Deluxe Coupe, Series D11   *Photo on page 49*

This coupe body by Hayes Body Corporation pioneered coupe styles with seating for four persons.

Length: 186 in. (472 cm)
Wheelbase: 117 in. (297 cm)
Weight: 3,075 lb. (1,395 kg)
Engine: Inline L-head six-cylinder
Transmission: Three-speed manual
Displacement: 217 cu. in. (3,294 cc)
Horsepower: 87
Cruising speed: 55 mph (88 km/h)
Price: $1,055

1956 Custom Royal Lancer *Photo on page 79*

This top-of-the-line model featured a push-button controlled automatic transmission. This model is equipped with the high-performance D-500 engine first offered this year.

Length: 212 in. (538 cm)
Wheelbase: 120 in. (305 cm)
Weight: 3,505 lb. (1,590 kg)
Engine: Hemi-head V-8, four-barrel carburetor
Transmission: Push-button three-speed Torqueflite automatic
Displacement: 315 cu. in. (5,163 cu cm)
Horsepower: 260
Cruising speed: 70+ mph (113 km/h)
Price: $2,693

1964 "Color Me Gone" Drag Car *Photo on page 94*

Reconstruction of one of the most famous of the limited edition drag cars. Quarter mile time: 11.7 seconds at 124 mph.

Length: 204.2 in. (519 cm)
Wheelbase: 117 in. (297 cm)
Weight: 3,255 lb. (1,475 kg)
Engine: V-8 wedge
Transmission: Push-button three-speed automatic
Displacement: 426 cu. in. (6,982 cu cm)
Horsepower: 500+
Price: N.A.

1969 Charger Daytona Sport Coupe *Photo on page 95*

First U.S. production car capable of 200 mph; developed with extensive wind-tunnel testing to enhance high-speed performance.

Length: 221 in. (561 cm)
Wheelbase: 117 in. (297 cm)
Weight: 3,700 lb. (1,678 kg)
Engine: V-8
Transmission: Three-speed Torqueflite automatic
Displacement: 440 cu. in. (7,212 cu cm)
Horsepower: 375
Cruising speed: 70+ mph (113 km/h)
Price: $4,100

1970 Challenger T/A Hardtop *Photo on page 91*

Only 1,000 of the T/A, the Challenger street version, were built. The high-performance R/T version was driven by Sam Posey in Trans-Am races.

Length: 192 in. (488 cm)
Wheelbase: 111 in. (282 cm)
Weight: 3,405 lb. (1,545 kg)
Engine: V-8 engine with "six-pack," three two-barrel carburetors
Transmission: Three-speed automatic
Displacement: 340 cu. in. (5,573 cu cm)
Horsepower: 290
Cruising speed: 70+ mph (113 km/h)
Price: $3,266

1989 Viper Concept *Photo on page 117*

The original concept from the 1989 Detroit Auto Show that led to the production of the Viper.

Length: 168 in. (427 cm)
Wheelbase: 89 in. (226 cm)
Engine: V-10
Transmission: Six-speed manual
Displacement: 488 cu. in. (8 liter)
Horsepower: 450
Cruising speed: 80+ mph (129 km/h)

1996 Dodge Stratus Super Touring Series Race Car JAT C002

In 1997, the PacWest Touring Car Group posted seven wins and 19 podium finishes to capture the overall Drivers Championship in the North American Super Touring Car series. The racing modified Dodge Stratus cars broke nearly every Super Touring Track record in the process; in qualification the cars captured 12 of 14 final pole positions.

Length: N.A.
Wheel base: N.A.
Engine: Four-cylinder, 16 valve, fuel-injected
Transmission: XTRAC six-speed sequential gearbox
Displacement: 2.0 liter
Horse power: N.A.
Cruising speed: N.A.
Price: N.A.

1965 A/FX Drag Car
"Altered wheel base factory experimental." Drag car capable of quarter mile in 9.53 seconds at 147.5 mph.

Length: 204.4 in. (517 cm)
Wheelbase: 110 in. (279 cm)
Weight: 2,600 lb. (1,182 kg)
Engine: Hemi V-8
Transmission: Four-speed manual
Displacement: 426 cu. in. (6,982 cu cm)
Horsepower: 600+
Price: N.A.

Dodge Trucks

1929 ½ Ton Pickup   *Photo on page 37*
The first pickup factory-built by Chrysler Corporation.

Length: 168 in. (427 cm)
Wheelbase: 109 in. (277 cm)
Weight: 1,900 lb. (862 kg)
Engine: Inline L-head four-cylinder
Transmission: Three-speed manual
Displacement: 175 cu. in. (2,868 cu cm)
Horsepower: 45
Cruising speed: 40 mph (65 km/h)
Price: $540

1934 ½ Ton Pickup   *Photo on page 55*
This year's pickups featured passenger car styling and were known as the "glamor series."

Length: 207 in. (526 cm)
Wheelbase: 111.25 in. (283 cm)
Weight: 2,465 lb. (1,118 kg)
Engine: Inline L-head six-cylinder
Transmission: Three-speed manual
Displacement: 201.3 cu. in. (3,299 cu cm)
Horsepower: 75
Cruising speed: 45 mph (73 km/h)
Price: $500

1937 ½ Ton Panel Truck   *Photo on page 130*
The "humpback" or double-level roofed panel truck first appeared in 1933 and continued in production until 1938. It provided space then, is a collectible now.

Length: 198 in. (503 cm)
Wheelbase: 116 in. (295 cm)
Weight: 2,975 lb. (1,349 kg)
Engine: Inline L-head six-cylinder
Transmission: Three-speed manual
Displacement: 218 cu. in. (3,573 cu cm)
Horsepower: 75
Cruising speed: 50 mph (81 km/h)
Price: $625

1940 ½ Ton Pickup   *Photo on page 75*
A new Dodge truck series appeared in 1939 and was dubbed "job-rated."

Length: 198 in. (503 cm)
Wheelbase: 116 in. (295 cm)
Weight: 2,925 lb. (1,325 kg)
Engine: Inline L-head six-cylinder
Transmission: Three-speed manual
Displacement: 201 cu. in. (3,299 cu cm)
Horsepower: 79
Cruising speed: 50 mph (81 km/h)
Price: $590

1941 4 X 4 Army Command Car   *Photo on page 65*
One of the half million military vehicles built by Dodge in World War II.

Length: 191 in. (485 cm)
Wheelbase: 116 in. (295 cm)
Weight: 5,070 lb. (2,300 kg)
Engine: Inline L-head six-cylinder
Transmission: Four-speed manual
Displacement: 230 cu. in. (3,770 cu cm)
Horsepower: 85
Cruising speed: 40 mph (65 km/h)
Price: N.A.

1949 ½ Ton Pickup   *Photo on page 75*
A new series of Dodge trucks with "pilot house" cabs appeared in 1948, first new trucks since 1939.

Length: 198 in. (502 cm)
Wheelbase: 108 in. (274 cm)
Weight: 3,275 lb. (1,486 kg)
Engine: Inline L-head six-cylinder
Transmission: Three-speed manual
Displacement: 217.8 cu. in. (3,570 cu cm)
Horsepower: 95
Cruising speed: 50 mph (81 km/h)
Price: $1,263

1954 Power Wagon ¾ Ton Truck *Photo on page 75*

Introduced in 1946, the domestic version of World War II's workhorse truck remained virtually unchanged until 1968.

Length: 216 in. (549 cm)
Wheelbase: 126 in. (320 cm)
Weight: 5,100 lb. (2,313 kg)
Engine: L-head six-cylinder
Transmission: Four-speed manual (synchromesh after 1953)
Displacement: 230 cu. in. (3,294 cu cm)
Horsepower: 99
Cruising speed: 45 mph (72 km/h)
Price: $2,307

1957 ½ Ton Sweptside Pickup *Photo on page 131*

Introduced to compete with the Ford Ranchero and the Chevrolet El Camino.

Length: 211 in. (536 cm)
Wheelbase: 116 in. (295 cm)
Weight: 3,425 lb. (1,554 kg)
Engine: OHV V-8
Transmission: Three-speed automatic
Displacement: 315 cu. in. (5,162 cu cm)
Horsepower: 204
Cruising speed: 60 mph (100 km/h)
Price: $1,614

1978 Li'l Red Express Pickup

Performance truck promoted as "adult toy" and fastest American production vehicle in 1978.

Length: 194 in. (493 cm)
Wheelbase: 114.5 in. (291 cm)
Weight: 3,695 lb. (1,676 kg)
Engine: V-8
Transmission: Performance automatic
Displacement: 360 cu. in. (5,900 cu cm)
Horsepower: 225
Cruising speed: 70+ mph (113 km/h)
Price: approx. $5,000

1964 Custom Sport Special Pickup

These sporty trucks included 50 equipped with a 426 cu. in. "street wedge" V-8; this is one.

Length: 214 in. (544 cm)
Wheelbase: 122 in. (310 cm)
Weight: 3,505 lb. (1,590 kg)
Engine: V-8 wedge
Transmission: Three-speed Loadflite automatic
Displacement: 426 cu. in. (6,982 cu cm)
Horsepower: 365
Cruising speed: 70+ mph (113 km/h)
Price: $1,823

1986 Rod Hall Baja Truck

A show version of the 4 X 4 truck Rod Hall used to capture the 1987 off-road championship.

Length: 198 in. (503 cm)
Wheelbase: 115 in. (292 cm)
Weight: N.A.
Engine: V-8
Transmission: Three-speed automatic
Displacement: 360 cu. in. (5,900 cu cm)
Horsepower: Not released
Price: N.A.

Eagle

1993 Vision *Photo on page 116*
One of three LH models that ushered in "cab-forward" design. Featured four-wheel disc brakes and four-wheel independent suspension.

Length: 150 in. (381 cm)
Wheelbase: 113 in. (287 cm)
Weight: 3,422 lb. (1,552 kg)
Engine: V-6, 24 valve
Transmission: Four-speed automatic
Displacement: 201 cu. in. (3.5 liter)
Horsepower: 214
Cruising speed: 70+ (113 km/h)
Price: N.A.

Jeep

1993 Grand Cherokee *Photo on page 115*
First luxury SUV and first SUV with a driver-side air bag. This vehicle was also the first vehicle produced by Chrysler's new Jefferson North plant.

Length: 177 in. (450 cm)
Wheelbase: 106.5 in. (271 cm)
Weight: 2,785 lb. (1,263 kg)
Engine: Inline six-cylinder
Transmission: Four-speed automatic, four-wheel drive
Displacement: 242 cu. in. (3,966 cu cm)
Horsepower: 190
Cruising speed: 70 mph (113 km/h)
Price: approx. $23,000

Plymouth

1928 Model Q Rumble-Seat Coupe *Photo on page 38*
Chrysler's entry into the low-priced field, the Plymouth was introduced in 1928. Initially known as the Chrysler-Plymouth, the vehicle was the only four-cylinder car in Chrysler's lineup.

Length: 168 in. (427 cm)
Wheelbase: 109.75 in. (279 cm)
Weight: 2,345 lb. (1,064 kg)
Engine: Inline L-head four-cylinder
Transmission: Three-speed manual
Displacement: 170.3 cu. in. (2,791 cu cm)
Horsepower: 45
Cruising speed: 45 mph (73 km/h)
Price: $720

1932 Model PB Convertible Sedan *Photo on page 47*
Without question, the PB represented the apex of Plymouth's four-cylinder car production.

Length: 175 in. (442 cm)
Wheelbase: 112 in. (284 cm)

Weight: 2,920 lb. (1,322 kg)
Engine: Inline four-cylinder
Transmission: Three-speed manual
Displacement: 196 cu. in. (3,212 cu cm)
Horsepower: 65
Cruising speed: 50 mph (80 km/h)
Price: $785

1957 Fury Hardtop Coupe *Photo on page 77*
Style, luxury and power were packaged in the special high-performance Fury offered in 1957.

Length: 206.1 in. (523 cm)
Wheelbase: 118 in. (300 cm)
Weight: 3,595 lb. (1,631 kg)
Engine: V-8 with polyspheric combustion chamber and two four-barrel carburetors
Transmission: Three-speed Torqueflite automatic
Displacement: 318 cu. in. (5,212 cu cm)
Horsepower: 290
Cruising speed: 70+ mph (113 km/h)
Price: $2,900

1960 Valiant V-200 4-Door Sedan *Photo on page 88*
Well-engineered compact introduced the slant-six engine and the first alternator in U.S.

Length: 188 in. (478 cm)
Wheelbase: 106.5 in. (271 cm)
Weight: 2,655 lb. (1,204 kg)
Engine: Inline slant-six with overhead valves
Transmission: Push-button three-speed Torqueflite automatic
Displacement: 170 cu. in. (2,786 cu cm)
Horsepower: 101
Cruising speed: 70+ mph (113 km/h)
Price: $2,130

1965 Barracuda Sport *Photo on page 92*
The Plymouth Barracuda actually beat the Ford Mustang to the market by a few weeks, inaugurating the "pony car" era.

Length: 188.2 in. (478 cm)
Wheelbase: 106 in. (269 cm)
Weight: 2,905 lb. (1,318 kg)
Engine: V-8
Transmission: Three-speed Torqueflite automatic
Displacement: 273 cu. in. (4,474 cu cm)
Horsepower: 180
Cruising speed: 70+ mph (113 km/h)
Price: $2,535

1969 Road Runner *Photo on page 93*
The 1969 *Motor Trend* Car of the Year. 44,599 sold. 0 to 60 in 7.0 seconds.

Length: 116 in. (295 cm)
Wheelbase: 115 in. (292 cm)
Weight: 3,405 lb. (1,548 kg)
Engine: V-8
Transmission: Four-speed manual

Displacement: 440 cu. in. (7,212 cu cm)
Horsepower: 390
Cruising speed: 70+ mph (113 km/h)
Price: about $4,000

1970 'Cuda Coupe   *Photo on page 92*

The 1970 Barracuda line offered three body styles and nine engines. Only 652 Hemi 'Cudas were built. One won the 1970 Pro Stock Championship.

Length: 186.7 in. (474 cm)
Wheelbase: 108 in. (274 cm)
Weight: 2,295 lb. (1,540 kg)
Engine: Hemi-head V-8 engine with two four-barrel carburetors
Transmission: Selective sliding gear four-speed
Displacement: 426 cu. in. (6,982 cu cm)
Horsepower: 425
Cruising speed: 70+ mph (113 km/h)
Price: $3,164 (approx. $871 for "street Hemi" package)

1970 Duster Coupe   *Photo on page 93*

This sporty compact fastback replaced the Valiant—a family car with sporty performance for a bargain price.

Length: 183.4 in. (479 cm)
Wheelbase: 108 in. (274 cm)
Weight: 3,110 lb. (1,410 kg)
Engine: OHV V-8 with hydraulic lifters
Transmission: Three-speed automatic
Displacement: 340 cu. in. (5,573 cu cm)
Horsepower: 275
Cruising speed: 70+ mph (113 km/h)
Price: $2,547 (slant-six version)

1978 Horizon Hatchback   *Photo on page 103*

The Horizon and twin Dodge Omni were the first U.S. subcompacts with front-wheel drive and transverse-mounted engines, patterned after the SIMCA Horizon.

Length: 162 in. (411 cm)
Wheelbase: 99.9 in. (252 cm)
Weight: 2,145 lb. (1,015 kg)
Engine: Transverse-mounted inline OHC four-cylinder
Transmission: Three-speed automatic Torqueflite
Displacement: 104.7 cu. in. (1,716 cu cm)
Horsepower: 75
Cruising speed: 70+ mph (113 km/h)
Price: $3,976

1981 Reliant Coupe   *Photo on page 111*

The "K-Car" twins, Plymouth Reliant and Dodge Aries, were Chrysler's first front-wheel-drive compacts. The K platform became the basis for all Chrysler cars for the next several years.

Length: 176 in. (447 cm)
Wheelbase: 99.6 in. (253 cm)
Weight: 2,305 lb. (1,046 kg)
Engine: Transverse-mounted, overhead cam, inline four-cylinder

Transmission: Three-speed Torqueflite
Displacement: 135 cu. in. (2,213 cu cm)
Horsepower: 84
Cruising speed: 70+ mph (113 km/h)
Price: $5,880

1984 Voyager Minivan   *Photo on page 112*

The domestic auto industry's first minivan featuring four-wheel drive was introduced in November 1983 and was an instant success. The Voyager and its Dodge twin, the Caravan, created a new market segment which they dominated for more than a decade.

Length: 176 in. (447 cm)
Wheelbase: 112 in. (284 cm)
Weight: 2,935 lb. (1,332 kg)
Engine: Transverse-mounted inline OHC four-cylinder
Transmission: Three-speed automatic
Displacement: 2.6 liter
Horsepower: 90
Cruising speed: 70+ mph (113 km/h)
Price: $8,280

Heritage Companies

AMC

1961 Metropolitan Convertible   *Photo on page 114*

Built in England by Austin, first for Nash, then AMC, from 1954 to 1960.

Length: 149.5 in. (240 cm)
Wheelbase: 85 in. (216 cm)
Weight: 1,890 lb. (857 kg)
Engine: OHV four-cylinder
Transmission: Three-speed manual
Displacement: 90 cu. in. (820 cu cm)
Horsepower: 52
Cruising speed: 50 mph (81 km/h)

1968 AMX   *Photo on page 93*

A two-seat sports car based on a shortened version of AMC's Javelin pony car.

Length: 177.2 in. (450 cm)
Wheelbase: 97 in. (246 cm)
Weight: 3,126 lb. (1,418 kg)
Transmission: Four-speed manual
Displacement: 390 cu. in. (6,392 cu cm)
Horsepower: 315
Cruising speed: 70+ mph (113 km/h)
Price: $3,395

Hudson

1909 Model 20 Three-Passenger Roadster *Photo on page 17*

The first Hudson left the factory on June 3, 1909. By the following July more than 4,000 Hudsons had been sold, largest first-year business recorded in the auto industry to that time.

Length: 144 in. (366 cm)
Wheelbase: 110 in. (280 cm)
Weight: 1,800 lb. (816 kg)
Engine: Inline four-cylinder
Transmission: Three-speed manual
Displacement: 198 cu. in. (3,248 cu cm)
Horsepower: 20
Cruising speed: 30 mph (50 km/h)
Price: $900

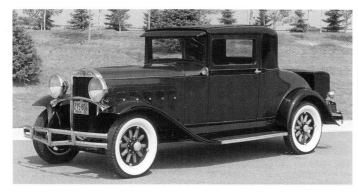

1930 Model T Coupe

First year of the Hudson Straight 8, which remained in production over 20 years. Year before Hudson was third in terms of sales.

Length: 175 in. (444 cm)
Wheelbase: 126 in. (320 cm)
Weight: 3,060 lb. (1,388 kg)
Engine: Inline L-head eight-cylinder
Transmission: Three-speed manual
Displacement: 213.8 cu. in. (3,504 cu cm)
Horsepower: 80
Cruising speed: 50 mph (81 km/h)
Price: $925

1953 Club Coupe *Photo on page 77*

Equipped with "severe usage" (racing) components including "Twin H Power"—two one-barrel carburetors—this car dominated NASCAR competition from 1951 to 1954.

Length: 208.5 in. (530 cm)
Wheelbase: 124 in. (315 cm)
Weight: 3,530 lb. (1,601 kg)
Engine: Inline L-head six-cylinder
Transmission: Three-speed with overdrive

Displacement: 308 cu. in. (5,505 cu cm)
Horsepower: 200+
Price: $2,742

Jeep (Heritage)

1943 Willys-Overland Model MB *Photo on page 66*

Willys and Ford (under license) built more than 600,000 during World War II, creating a reputation that made a successful transition to a civilian brand.

Length: 131 in. (332 cm)
Wheelbase: 80 in. (203 cm)
Weight: 2,453 lb. (1,113 kg)
Engine: Inline L-head four cylinder "Go Devil"
Transmission: Three-speed manual with transfer case, auxiliary gearbox and high- and low-range for four-wheel drive
Displacement: 134 cu. in (2,196 cu cm)
Horsepower: 65
Cruising speed: 45 mph (73 km/h)

1945 Willys-Overland Model CJ-2A *Photo on page 67*

Willys-Overland made the decision to build everything based on Jeep after the war. This is a very early civilian version Jeep.

Length: 130 in. (330 cm)
Wheelbase: 80 in. (203 cm)
Weight: 2,037 lb. (924 kg)
Engine: Inline L-head four cylinder
Transmission: Three-speed manual with transfer case, auxiliary gear box and high- and low-range for four-wheel drive
Displacement: 134.2 cu. in. (2,220 cu cm)
Horsepower: 65
Cruising speed: 45 mph (73 km/h)
Price: $1,090

1949 Willys-Overland Model 4 x 463 Station Wagon *Photo on page 68*

Introduced in 1946 with rear-wheel drive as the first all-steel station wagon intended for the noncommercial market. Four-wheel drive added in 1949 made this the direct antecedent of the SUV.

Length: 174 in. (442 cm)
Wheelbase: 104 in. (264 cm)
Weight: 3,136 lb. (1,422 kg)
Engine: Inline L-head four-cylinder
Transmission: Three-speed manual with transfer case, auxiliary gear box, and high- and low-range four-wheel drive
Displacement: 134.2 cu. in. (2,200 cu cm)
Horsepower: 69
Cruising speed: 50 mph (81 km/h)
Price: $1,875

1950 Willys-Overland Model 450 First Series Jeepster Phaeton *Photo on page 67*

Built on the station wagon chassis, the Jeepster was another effort to broaden Jeep's market, in this case with a sporty recreational vehicle.

Length: 174.8 in. (444 cm)
Wheelbase: 104 in. (264 cm)
Weight: 2,468 lb. (1,110 kg)
Engine: Inline F-head four-cylinder
Transmission: Three-speed manual
Displacement: 134.2 cu. in. (2,200 cu cm)
Horsepower: 63
Cruising speed: 50 mph (81 km/.h)
Price: $1,495

1973 AMC CJ-5 Model 83 *Photo on page 67*

First Jeep offering a V-8.

Length: 138.75 in. (352 cm)
Wheelbase: 84 in. (213 cm)
Weight: 2,450 lb. (1,109 kg)
Engine: OHV V-8
Transmission: Three-speed manual
Displacement: 304 cu. in. (4,983 cu cm)
Horsepower: 150
Cruising speed: 60 mph (100 km/h)
Price: $3,086

Nash

1902 Rambler Model C Runabout *Photo on page 16*

This is an example of the first Rambler models offered to the public by Thomas Jeffrey. A total of 1,500 Ramblers were produced in 1902, making it the second mass-produced vehicle in the world, behind Oldsmobile.

Length: 108 in. (274 cm)
Wheelbase: 78 in. (198 cm)
Weight: 1,200 lb. (544 kg)
Engine: One-cylinder water-cooled
Transmission: Chain drive
Displacement: N.A.
Horsepower: 4
Cruising speed: 14 mph (23 km/h)
Price: $750

1929 Model 440 Sedan

First year of Nash OHV engine fitted with twin ignition, a Nash hallmark until 1940.

Length: 197 in. (500 cm)
Wheelbase: 116 in. (295 cm)
Weight: 3,400 lb. (1,542 kg)
Engine: Inline OHV six-cylinder, twin ignition
Transmission: Three-speed manual
Displacement: 224 cu. in. (3,671 cu cm)
Horsepower: 65
Cruising speed: 45 mph (73 km/h)
Price: $1,345

1953 Nash Healey

"Image car" introduced with Nash drive train, English Healey running gear and Pinin Farina body.

Length: 170.75 in. (434 cm)
Wheelbase: 102 in. (259 cm)
Weight: 2,500 lb. (1,134 kg)
Engine: Inline OHV six-cylinder
Transmission: Three-speed manual
Displacement: 252.6 cu. in. (4,140 cu cm)
Horsepower: 125
Cruising speed: 60 mph (97 km/h)
Price: $5,128

Willys

1917 Willys Knight Model 88-8 Touring *Photo on page 27*

Prestige product of Willys, then second largest automaker in world. Willys was biggest maker of Knight engines. This is a rare V-8 with dual exhausts and rear transaxle.

Length: 173 in. (439 cm)
Wheelbase: 123 in. (312 cm)
Weight: approx. 4,000 lb. (1,811 kg)
Engine: Sleeve value V-8
Transmission: Three-speed manual rear transaxle
Displacement: 286 cu. in. (4,688 cu cm)
Horsepower: 65
Cruising speed: 40 mph (65 km/h)
Price: $1,950

WALTER P. CHRYSLER MUSEUM
Forward: The American Heritage of DaimlerChrysler

First printing. Printed in U.S.A.

ISBN 0-9709952-0-2

Produced by ZENDA INC.:

Written by Charles Phillips, *Editor*
Edited by Candace Floyd, *Managing Editor*
Designed by Bruce Gore, *Gore Studio, Inc.*

Picture Credits. *Images in this book are courtesy DaimlerChrysler Corporation except for the following images, listed by source, page number and (in parentheses) the position of the image on page where called for.* **AFP-Uniphoto**: 126 (timeline); **AP/World Wide Photos**: 45, 82 (timeline), 93 (timeline), 96, 122 (timeline), Paul Watson/*Toronto Star*/AP—124 (timeline, bottom); **Ben Martin**: 76 (timeline, bottom); **Bettmann/CORBIS**: 15, 39 (timeline, top), 44, 55 (timeline, bottom), 74 (timeline, top), 76 (timeline, top), 94 (timeline), 100, 102, 105 (timeline), AFP/CORBIS—131 (timeline, top), DaimlerChrysler through CORBIS digital stock—2, © Randy Faris/CORBIS—87, Reuters/CORBIS—127 (timeline), © Jaques Langevin/ SYGMA/CORBIS—120, Underwood & Underwood/CORBIS—27 (timeline, top), UPI/CORBIS—64 (timeline, top); **Black Star**: Eugene Smith/Black Star—61 (timeline, bottom), © 1963 Fred Ward Prod., Inc./Black Star—90 (timeline), © Joseph Rodriquez/Black Star—106, Steve Shapiro/Black Star—102 (timeline); **Bostwick-Frohardt Collection, Owned by KMTV, Omaha Nebr.**: 20; **Brown Brothers**: 12, 26 (timeline), 27 (timeline, bottom); 36 (timeline, bottom), 38 (timeline, top), 53 (timeline); from *Chrysler in Competition* by **Ray Jones and Martin Swing**: 41(both); *Collectible Automobile Magazine* ®/**Publications International, Ltd.**: 74 (lower left; bottom), 76 (upper right), 101 (top); **Contact Press Images**: David Burnett/Contact Press—110 (timeline, top), © Sebastio Salgada/Contact Press—111 (timeline, bottom); **Dale Wittner**: 116 (timeline); **Detroit Public Library**: Burton Historical Collection—16 (left), National Automotive Historical Collection—17 (timeline), 19 (timeline), 24 (inset), 25 (timeline), 34 (timeline), 36 (timeline, top), 40 (timeline, top), 50 (timeline, bottom); **Ernest C. Withers courtesy Panoptican Gallery, Boston Mass.**: 79 (timeline, bottom); **Getty**: Terry Ashe/Gamma/Liason Agency—115 (timeline, top), Tim Parker/Archive Photos—131 (timeline, bottom); **Heinrich Hoffman**: 48 (timeline); **Henry Ford Museum**: 18 (timeline); © **Ira Wyman**: 121; **Irving Penn, Courtesy *Vogue* Magazine**: 67 (timeline, bottom); © **Jerry Gay**: 98; **Jim Arso/SABA**: 128 (timeline); **John P. Filo**: 100 (timeline, top); **J. R. Eyerman**: 70; **Library of Congress**: 14, 24 (timeline), 28, 38 (timeline, bottom), 39 (timeline, bottom), 42, 47 (timeline, bottom), 52 (timeline); **Louis Sanchez**: 83 (timeline, bottom); **Magnum Photos, Inc.**: Alex Webb/ Magnum—103 (timeline, top),

Burt Gunn/Magnum—83 (timeline, top), 101, Robert Capa/Magnum—63 (timeline, top), Stuart Franklin/Magnum—117 (timeline, top); **Margaret C. Gladbach Trust**: 52 (bottom); **Michael Ochs Archives**: 88 (timeline, top), 99; **Michigan State Archives**: 17 (inset); **Movie Still Archives, Harrison, Nebr.**: 104 (timeline); **NASA**: 84, 95 (timeline, top), 112 (timeline), 115 (timeline, bottom), 130 (timeline); **National Archives**: 23, 32 (timeline), 55 (timeline, top), 56, 58, 62 (timeline, top), 63 (timeline, bottom), 65 (timeline, bottom), 74 (timeline, bottom), 77 (timeline, bottom), 88 (timeline, bottom); © **Neil Liefer**: 108; **Nikolas Murray**: 33 (timeline, top), 51 (timeline, top); *from A Pictorial History of Jazz* **by Orrin Keeprews and Bill Grauer, Jr.**: 41 (timeline, top); **Security National Bank, Los Angeles: Historical Collections**: 22; **SIPA Press**: Manoocher/ SIPA—110 (timeline, bottom), Randy Brandon/SIPA—117 (timeline, bottom); **Stephen Shames/Matrix**: 109; © **Time, Inc.**: 111 (timeline, top), Alfred Eisenstadt/*Life* Magazine—65 (timeline, top), Arthur Schatz/*Life* Magazine—92 (timeline, bottom), Cynthia Johnson/TimePix—124 (timeline, top), Co Rentmeister/*Life* Magazine—101 (timeline, bottom), Hy Deskin/*Life* Magazine—67 (timeline, top), Margaret Bourke-White/*Life* Magazine—46 (timeline, top), 64 (timeline, bottom), Michael Mauney/*Life* Magazine—103 (timeline, bottom), Walter Sanders/*Life* Magazine—69 (timeline); © **Tom Miner, The Image Works, Woodstock, New York**: 95 (timeline, bottom); **Union Pacific Museum Collection**: 19 (bottom); **William F. Warneck/CBS Photo Archive**: 81 (timeline, bottom).

WALTER P. CHRYSLER MUSEUM
One Chrysler Drive CIMS 488.00.00
Auburn Hills, Michigan 48326-2778
Museum Manager: Barry Dressel
Corporate Historical Collection Manager: Brandt Rosenbusch
Telephone: 1-888-456-1924
www.chryslerheritage.com